Collins
PRIMARY HISTORY

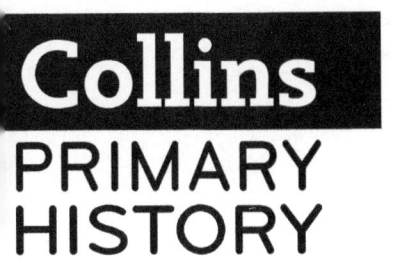

Teacher's Guide

Sue Temple | Alf Wilkinson

William Collins' dream of knowledge for all began with the publication of his first book in 1819.
A self-educated mill worker, he not only enriched millions of lives, but also founded a flourishing publishing house. Today, staying true to this spirit, Collins books are packed with inspiration, innovation and practical expertise. They place you at the centre of a world of possibility and give you exactly what you need to explore it.

Collins. Freedom to teach.

Published by Collins
An imprint of HarperCollins*Publishers*
The News Building
1 London Bridge Street
London
SE1 9GF
www.harpercollins.co.uk
HarperCollins*Publishers*
1st Floor, Watermarque Building, Ringsend Road
Dublin 4, Ireland

Browse the complete Collins catalogue at
www.collins.co.uk

© HarperCollins*Publishers* Limited 2019

Map © Collins Bartholomew 2019

10 9 8 7 6 5

ISBN 978-0-00-831087-5

All rights reserved. No part of this publication may be reproduced, stored in a retrieval system, or transmitted in any form by any means, electronic, mechanical, photocopying, recording or otherwise, without the prior written permission of the Publisher or a licence permitting restricted copying in the United Kingdom issued by the Copyright Licensing Agency Ltd, Barnard's Inn, 86 Fetter Lane, London, EC4A 1EN.

British Library Cataloguing-in-Publication Data
A catalogue record for this publication is available from the British Library.

Authors: Sue Temple and Alf Wilkinson
Publisher: Lizzie Catford
Product developer: Natasha Paul
Copyeditor: Sally Clifford
Proofreader: Kim Vernon
Map designer: Gordon MacGilp
Cover designer and illustrator: Steve Evans
Typesetter: Jouve India Private Ltd
Production controller: Rachel Weaver
Printed and Bound in the UK using 100% Renewable Electricity at CPI Group (UK) Ltd

MIX
Paper from responsible sources
FSC C007454
www.fsc.org
This book is produced from independently certified FSC™ paper to ensure responsible forest management.

For more information visit:
www.harpercollins.co.uk/green

The publishers gratefully acknowledge the permission granted to reproduce the copyright material in this book. Every effort has been made to trace copyright holders and to obtain their permission for the use of copyright material. The publishers will gladly receive any information enabling them to rectify any error or omission at the first opportunity.

p29 Rambleon/Shutterstock; p30tl TierneyMJ/Shutterstock; p30tr Lipowski Milan/Shutterstock; p30cl JoeClemson/Shutterstock; p30cr Vereshchagin Dmitry/Shutterstock; p30bl Mr Doomits/Shutterstock; p30br Voronin76/Shutterstock; p40t Artexplorer/Alamy Stock Photo; p40c Granger Historical Picture Archive/Alamy Stock Photo; p40b INTERFOTO/Alamy Stock Photo; p42 The Wreck of HMS Birkenhead off the Cape of Good Hope on 26 Feb. 1852, 1892 (litho) (later colouration), Hemy, Thomas Marie Madawaska (1852-1937)/The Argory, County Armagh, Northern Ireland/Bridgeman Images; p54 World History Archive/Alamy Stock Photo; p56tl American Photo Archive/Alamy Stock Photo; p56tr Everett Collection Inc/Alamy Stock Photo; p56bl Alpha Historica/Alamy Stock Photo; p56br PictureLux/The Hollywood Archive/Alamy Stock Photo; p66l robertharding/Alamy Stock Photo; p66r Ivana Drljan/Alamy Stock Photo; p89 Pictorial Press Ltd/Alamy Stock Photo; p91 Granger Historical Picture Archive/Alamy Stock Photo; p92 Chronicle/Alamy Stock Photo; p93 tatianasun/Shutterstock; p106 © The Trustees of the British Museum; p114 George Atsametakis/Alamy Stock Photo; p134l ©HarperCollinsPublishers; p134r ©HarperCollinsPublishers.

We are grateful to the following for permission to reproduce copyright material:

An extract from 'Vikings History: An Overview of the Culture and History of the Viking Age,' History on the Net, https://www.historyonthenet.com/vikings-history-overview-culture-history-viking-age, accessed 17/06/2019. Reproduced with permission; and an extract from *Egyptian Women: Life in Ancient Egypt* by Caroline Seawright, copyright © 2001, http://www.thekeep.org/~kunoichi/kunoichi/themestream/women_egypt.html. Reproduced with kind permission.

All weblinks were correct at the time of publication.

Contents

Introduction to the series	5
About the series	6
Learning objectives matching grid	8
The purpose of studying history	9
Skills in history	11
What do pupils find difficult about history?	14
What does it mean to get better at history?	20
Where to find out more	21

Teaching history to pupils aged 5–7

Changes Within Living Memory	**23**
Overview of Pupil Book contents	24
Timeline	25
Knowledge organiser and skills grid	26
Teaching about changes within living memory to pupils aged 5–7	27
Resource sheets	29
Pupil Book model answers	32
Events Beyond Living Memory	**33**
Overview of Pupil Book contents	34
Timeline	35
Knowledge organiser and skills grid	36
Teaching about events beyond living memory to pupils aged 5–7	37
Resource sheets	39
Pupil Book model answers	45
Significant Individuals	**46**
Overview of Pupil Book contents	47
Timeline	48
Knowledge organiser and skills grid	49
Teaching about significant individuals to pupils aged 5–7	50
Resource sheets	52
Pupil Book model answers	57

Teaching history to pupils aged 7–11

Stone Age to Iron Age	**59**
Topic introduction	60
Overview of Pupil Book contents	61
Knowledge organiser and skills grid	62
Additional resources	63
Getting better at history	64
Resource sheets	65
Pupil Book model answers	70

HarperCollins*Publishers* 2019

Invaders	**71**	Additional resources	101
Topic introduction	72	Getting better at history	102
Overview of Pupil Book contents	73	Resource sheets	103
Knowledge organiser and skills grid	74	Pupil Book model answers	107
Additional resources	75	**Ancient Greece**	**109**
Getting better at history	76	Topic introduction	110
Resource sheets	77	Overview of Pupil Book contents	111
Pupil Book model answers	82	Knowledge organiser and skills grid	112
Victorian Times	**84**	Additional resources	113
Topic introduction	85	Getting better at history	114
Overview of Pupil Book contents	86	Resource sheets	115
Knowledge organiser and skills grid	87	Pupil Book model answers	120
Additional resources	88	**The Maya**	**122**
Getting better at history	89	Topic introduction	123
Resource sheets	91	Overview of Pupil Book contents	124
Pupil Book model answers	95	Knowledge organiser and skills grid	125
Ancient Egypt	**97**	Additional resources	126
Topic introduction	98	Getting better at history	127
Overview of Pupil Book contents	99	Resource sheets	128
Knowledge organiser and skills grid	100	Pupil Book model answers	135

HarperCollins*Publishers* 2019

Introduction to the series

The key idea behind this series is to make history exciting for both teachers and learners. There is currently a lot of discussion about the knowledge-based curriculum, but good history uses both knowledge and skills together, although historical knowledge often changes as more evidence emerges or new ways of looking at old ideas develop. That is one of the most exciting things about studying history – it does not stay the same. A perfect example of this is the recent discovery of Must Farm, near Peterborough, now known as 'Britain's Pompeii', where a burned-down Bronze Age village has forced archaeologists to re-think their ideas about life during the Bronze Age. Recent discoveries have changed lots of the ideas historians have about many of the topics in these books!

Each book has a knowledge checklist – the 'Key Facts', that pupils ought to know about the topic. These give a knowledge framework to help understand the topic better. One of the hardest things in history is how to develop a sense of the past – what was it really like to live in, for example, Victorian times. This is much more than knowing most people lived in towns and worked in factories; worked long hours for low pay; that housing conditions were bad. You can only develop this sense of the past if you ask questions such as 'Why was it like this?', not just 'What was it like?'

Each unit is designed to help pupils develop at least one of the skills needed to become good historians such as weighing up evidence, thinking about continuity and change, understanding why historians come to different conclusions about key events in history. Each of these is spelled out in the 'skills grid' in each book. Getting better at using these skills is an integral part of getting better at history. They each help us make sense of the evidence we find about life in the past and, like the times tables, need frequent re-visiting to reinforce learning.

Perhaps the hardest thing for pupils to comprehend is the fact that often there is no one correct answer to many history questions. The answer you arrive at usually depends on the evidence you use. That is why so many of the activities in these books are open-ended, to help pupils reach their own conclusions based on the evidence they have. We have really enjoyed thinking about these things and writing these books. We hope your pupils enjoy using them.

Alf Wilkinson and Sue Temple

About the series

Welcome to the Collins Primary History Teacher's Guide

Welcome to the Collins Primary History Teacher's Guide. This guide offers guidance for covering each of the Pupil Books. For each of the nine Pupil Books, there is a clear structure of teacher guidance, with an overview of the Pupil Book's contents, a knowledge organiser, a skills grid, teaching ideas, photocopiable resource sheets and support for assessing answers to questions in the Pupil Books. The resource sheets for topics aimed at pupils aged 5–7 are designed with notes for the teachers at the bottom, which can be cut out before distributing to pupils. The resource sheets for topics aimed at pupils aged 7–11 can be used to structure answers to questions in the Pupil Books. Model answers are included to demonstrate things to look out for in pupils' work.

Pupil Books

The Pupil Books offer a clear structure and easy-to-follow design to help learners to navigate the topic. Each book focuses on one historical topic, and includes clear headings to organise the content, and interesting maps and images to support the text.

There are three books aimed at pupils aged 5–7, and six books aimed at pupils aged 7–11.

Pupil Books for ages 5–7

Each of the three Pupil Books aimed at pupils aged 5–7 begin with a 'Getting started' unit, which includes an introduction to the topic aimed at the pupils, a timeline of key events that are covered within the book, and a world map. A combined timeline is also included at the back of these books, which demonstrates how the key events in all three Key Stage 1 topics fit together.

The material in each book has been organised into eight main units, each based on one key individual, event or aspect of the topic.

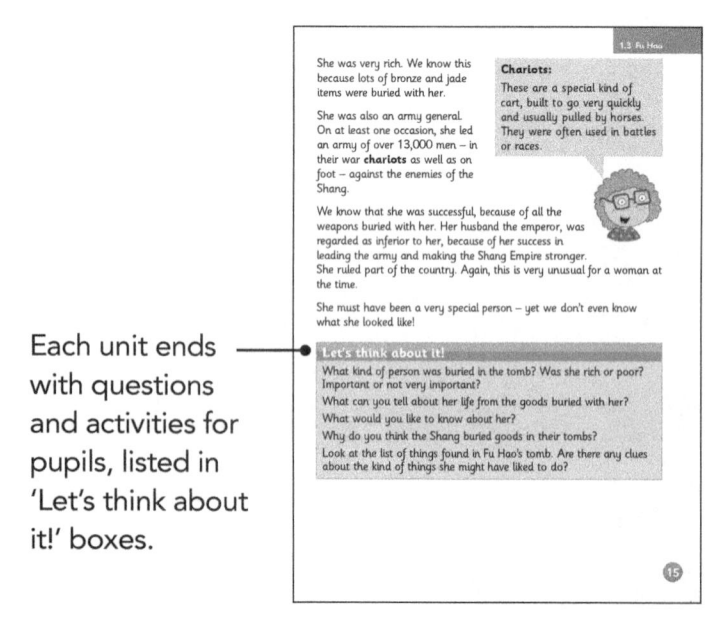

Each unit ends with questions and activities for pupils, listed in 'Let's think about it!' boxes.

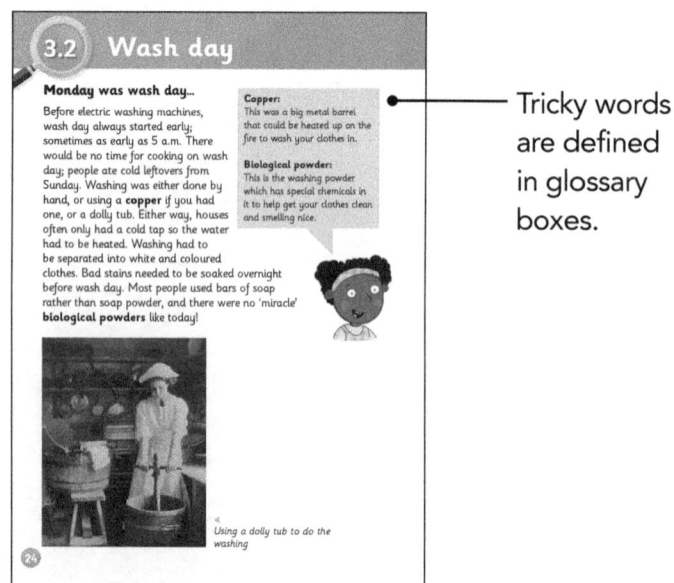

Tricky words are defined in glossary boxes.

HarperCollinsPublishers 2019

Pupil Books for ages 7–11

The material in each of the six Pupil Books aimed at pupils aged 7–11 has been organised into nine units, each based on one key aspect of the topic. A world map is included towards the end of these six Pupil Books.

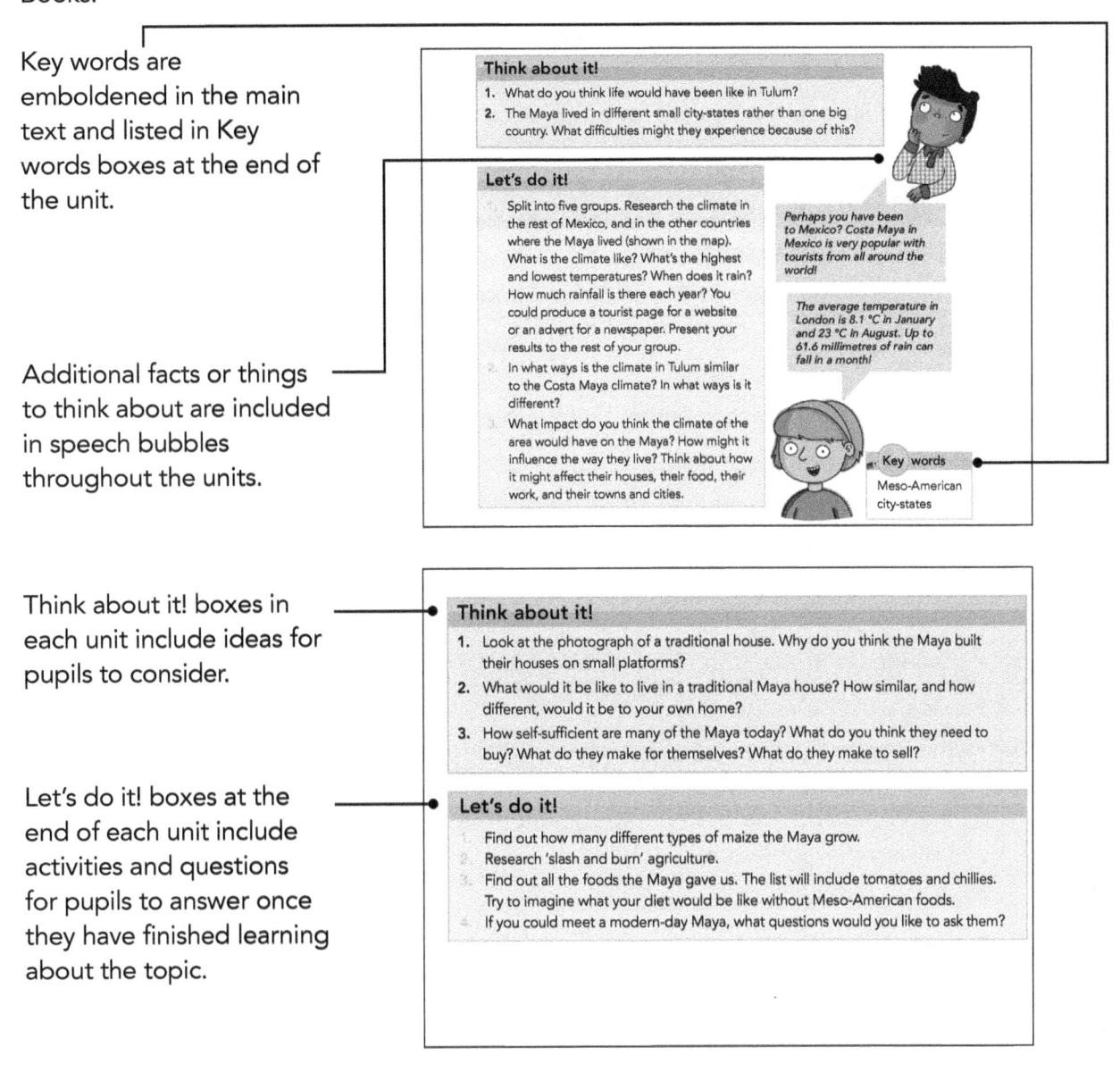

Key words are emboldened in the main text and listed in Key words boxes at the end of the unit.

Think about it!
1. What do you think life would have been like in Tulum?
2. The Maya lived in different small city-states rather than one big country. What difficulties might they experience because of this?

Let's do it!
Split into five groups. Research the climate in the rest of Mexico, and in the other countries where the Maya lived (shown in the map). What is the climate like? What's the highest and lowest temperatures? When does it rain? How much rainfall is there each year? You could produce a tourist page for a website or an advert for a newspaper. Present your results to the rest of your group.
In what ways is the climate in Tulum similar to the Costa Maya climate? In what ways is it different?
What impact do you think the climate of the area would have on the Maya? How might it influence the way they live? Think about how it might affect their houses, their food, their work, and their towns and cities.

Perhaps you have been to Mexico? Costa Maya in Mexico is very popular with tourists from all around the world!

The average temperature in London is 8.1 °C in January and 23 °C in August. Up to 61.6 millimetres of rain can fall in a month!

Additional facts or things to think about are included in speech bubbles throughout the units.

Key words
Meso-American
city-states

Think about it! boxes in each unit include ideas for pupils to consider.

Think about it!
1. Look at the photograph of a traditional house. Why do you think the Maya built their houses on small platforms?
2. What would it be like to live in a traditional Maya house? How similar, and how different, would it be to your own home?
3. How self-sufficient are many of the Maya today? What do you think they need to buy? What do they make for themselves? What do they make to sell?

Let's do it! boxes at the end of each unit include activities and questions for pupils to answer once they have finished learning about the topic.

Let's do it!
1. Find out how many different types of maize the Maya grow.
2. Research 'slash and burn' agriculture.
3. Find out all the foods the Maya gave us. The list will include tomatoes and chillies. Try to imagine what your diet would be like without Meso-American foods.
4. If you could meet a modern-day Maya, what questions would you like to ask them?

All nine of the Pupil Books end with a glossary of key terms and an index.

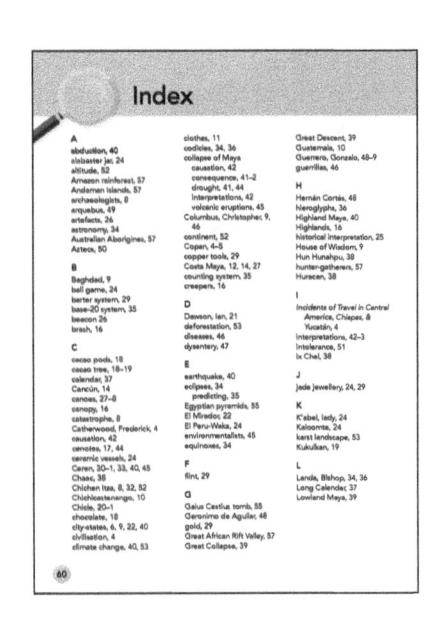

HarperCollins*Publishers* 2019

Learning objectives matching grid

The learning objectives from the National Curriculum for England covered in each book are listed here for easy reference.

Pupil Book title	National Curriculum for England learning objective
Changes Within Living Memory	Pupils should be taught about: • changes within living memory. Where appropriate, these should be used to reveal aspects of change in national life.
Events Beyond Living Memory	Pupils should be taught about: • events beyond living memory that are significant nationally or globally.
Significant Individuals	Pupils should be taught about: • the lives of significant individuals in the past who have contributed to national and international achievements. Some should be used to compare aspects of life in different periods.
Stone Age to Iron Age	Pupils should be taught about: • changes in Britain from the Stone Age to the Iron Age.
Invaders	Pupils should be taught about: • the Roman Empire and its impact on Britain • Britain's settlement by Anglo-Saxons and Scots • the Viking and Anglo-Saxon struggle for the Kingdom of England to the time of Edward the Confessor.
Victorian Times	Pupils should be taught about: • a study of an aspect or theme in British history that extends pupils' chronological knowledge beyond 1066.
Ancient Egypt	Pupils should be taught about: • the achievements of the earliest civilisations – an overview of where and when the first civilisations appeared and a depth study of one of the following: Ancient Sumer; The Indus Valley; Ancient Egypt; The Shang Dynasty of Ancient China.
Ancient Greece	Pupils should be taught about: • Ancient Greece – a study of Greek life and achievements and their influence on the western world.
The Maya	Pupils should be taught about: • a non-European society that provides contrasts with British history – one study chosen from: early Islamic civilisation, including a study of Baghdad c. 900 CE; Mayan civilisation c. 900 CE; Benin (West Africa) c. 900–1300 CE.

HarperCollins*Publishers* 2019

The purpose of studying history

The English National Curriculum for history starts with this paragraph about the purpose of studying the subject. We think it makes a brilliant manifesto around which to plan our teaching and learning:

> **The purpose of studying history**
>
> A high-quality history education will help pupils gain *a coherent knowledge and understanding* of Britain's past and that of the wider world. It *should inspire pupils' curiosity* to know more about the past. Teaching should equip pupils to *ask perceptive questions, think critically, weigh evidence, sift arguments, and develop perspective and judgement.* History helps pupils to *understand the complexity* of people's lives, *the process of change*, the *diversity of societies* and relationships between different groups, as well as *their own identity* and the challenges of their time.
>
> *(Department for Education, 2013; italics are those of the author)*

If we can help our pupils to achieve all this, then they will have a brilliant history education! Of course, the activities have to be age specific, and revisited over time to allow the skills to develop fully.

Younger children are just beginning to understand that there was a time before they were born, and so they need lots of activities which help them to grasp this – understanding that their grandparents were once small children is a big step at this age so activities such as talking to a real person about their school days, holidays or the food they ate are important steps towards this understanding. They may struggle to appreciate that some people and events were real and others are fiction, so learning about real people and real events from the past, what happened and why we remember them should be key aspects of your curriculum.

You might find it easier to keep a check on these aspirations using a planning grid a bit like this:

Pupils aged 5–7

Identified aim of history teaching	Where I do it when teaching Changes Within Living Memory	Where I do it when teaching Events Beyond Living Memory	Where I do it when teaching Significant Individuals
Use a wide range of everyday historical terms			
Understand that we use evidence to find out about the past			
Begin to evaluate sources (3 Rs)			
Ask and answer questions			
Identify similarities/differences between ways of life at different times			
Recognise why people did things, why events happened and what happened as a result			

HarperCollins*Publishers* 2019

Make simple observations about for example objects, buildings and people			
Talk about who is important and why for example in a simple historical account			
Use a wide range of everyday historical terms			
Understand the process of change			
Understand the diversity of societies			
Understand their own identity			
Understand the challenges of their time			

Pupils aged 7–11

Identified aim of history teaching	Example of where I do it in my lessons	Ranking
Coherent knowledge of their country's past		
Coherent knowledge of world history		
Inspire curiosity		
Ask perceptive questions		
Think critically		
Weigh evidence		
Sift arguments		
Develop perspective and judgement		
Understand the complexity of people's lives		
Understand the process of change		
Understand the diversity of societies		
Understand their own identity		
Understand the challenges of their time		

Skills in history

This table shows the skills and concepts that are especially important in studying history. History is not just about facts and dates – it also involves doing something with the information we have discovered. Each unit in each book in this history course focuses on at least one of these skills and concepts; helping your pupils to practise and develop each skill and concept in turn. The specific skill/concept targeted by each unit is always highlighted in a 'skills grid' at the end of Unit 8.

Chronological knowledge and understanding (including a sense of period)	Continuity and change in and between periods
Historical terms	Cause and consequence
Historical enquiry – Using evidence and Communicating ideas	Similarity/difference within a period/situation
Interpretations of history	Significance of events and/or people

Chronological knowledge and understanding

This helps pupils remember the duration and sequence of events in any topic they are studying, and what was happening at the same time in other periods they have studied. Good examples of this are looking at Rosa Parks in the Significant Individuals book and Unit 1.3 in the Maya topic book.

Continuity and change in and between periods

We tend to be very good at identifying **change** in history but sometimes tend to forget that many things **stayed the same**. Completing the School Comparison chart in the Changes Within Living Memory book shows how some things change and some things don't. Unit 3 in the Stone Age to Iron Age topic book emphasises that throughout this very long period of history many things stayed more or less the same, despite the changes from stone tools to bronze to iron. It is always worth asking 'What has stayed the same?'

Historical terms

Like any other subject, history has its own specialist vocabulary that pupils need to understand and to be able to use accurately. Words such as 'castle,' 'democracy' or 'empire' have very specific meanings, even if those meanings do change over time! When we are planning a study unit we ought to decide which words are appropriate for that unit, and ensure that we use then in context so the pupils get a chance to learn them and to understand them. Here is a selection of history words to start with – we're sure you can add more of your own!

yesterday	today	tomorrow	next
first	last	day	month
year	before	after	then
now	old	older	oldest
new	newer	newest	annual
empire	colony	BCE	CE
decade	century	monarch	agriculture
monastery	castle	church	prehistory

HarperCollins*Publishers* 2019

pope	long ago	dark ages	Bronze Age
Stone Age	discovery	archaeology	artefact
change	hunter-gatherer	interpretation	local
sacrifice	settler	significance	source
era	nomad	primary evidence	secondary evidence
museum	myth	legend	story
continuity	slave	lifetime	invader
Iron Age			

Cause and consequence

Pupils tend to believe that most things in history were inevitable – because they happened then they were bound to happen. This, of course, is not usually the case. Things happen for a reason – if the Romans had not left Britain, for example, would the Anglo-Saxons have come and settled there? And don't forget consequence – something that happened as a direct result of an action. Again, the Anglo Saxons lived in villages rather than towns so, as a result of them moving to England, cities largely disappeared, at least to begin with. Unit 8 in the Ancient Egypt topic book explores the causes and consequences of the discovery of Tutankhamun's tomb.

Historical enquiry – Using evidence and communicating ideas

Enquiry is at the heart of all good history – the search to discover evidence and to use that evidence to produce **an** answer to a valid historical question. Remember, not all answers to the same question will be the same! A good history enquiry has several stages:

1. Choosing a stimulating question to explore
2. Gathering evidence
3. Assessing the evidence
4. Making a judgement and coming to a conclusion – answering the question
5. Finally, communicating what you have discovered – there are many ways to present your conclusion – it does not have to be in writing!

Unit 5 in the Ancient Greece topic book is an example of an enquiry based on evidence and asking pupils to reach a conclusion and then present that in a meaningful way.

Similarity/difference within a period/situation

This is a really useful skill for exploring change, and for linking any period being studied with the present day. 'How is this similar to today?' 'How is it different?' are perfect questions to begin exploring what the topic you are studying was like. Unit 2, for example, in the Ancient Greece topic book, asks pupils to explore food then and now.

Interpretations of history

Children of this age find it difficult to understand that it is perfectly possible to have different views of an event or a person. Neither view is necessarily right or wrong – it just depends on what evidence you use to support your view. History is not an absolute, like, for example, science. Every time you heat up water, it turns into steam. In history, people act differently and respond to the same situation in different ways. This means that it is very common to find differing views of events, either by historians or people writing at the time – it all depends on your perspective and the evidence you use. Unit 7 in the Maya topic book explores the different ideas historians have about what happened to the Maya around about 900 CE – everyone agrees there was a huge change in Maya cities and life, but few agree on why this happened.

Significance of events and/or people

This is all about what makes something or someone very special – special enough to study in history. What makes this particular event so important? And if it was important at the time, is it still important today? Unit 1 in the Victorian Times topic book explores the significance of the Great Exhibition in 1851. Why was it held? What was it meant to do? Why do we still remember it today?

What do pupils find difficult about history?

There are several misunderstandings and confusions that affect pupils' progress in history. These include:

1. Chronology/change – anachronism and no sense of duration
2. Insufficient knowledge, resulting in simplistic and naive history
3. A limited understanding of why things happened and turned out as they did, including the role that human beings played in making things happen
4. Not really grasping how sources can be used properly
5. Struggling to accept that there can be several ways of looking at things in history (interpretations)
6. Pupils not understanding what teachers are asking them to do.

Confusion 1: Chronology/change – anachronism and no sense of duration

Without a sound grasp of the sequence and duration of events, history can appear disjointed and episodic. Good history requires a sense of what belongs in different periods and societies and being able to use the conventions for discriminating between periods of history.

What are some of the characteristics of this confusion?

- Ancient scenes with modern technology, mixing societies and features
- No sense of how much time has passed between events
- Periods such as Egyptian, Greek, Roman are taken as fixed and unchanging rather than dynamic and evolving
- Lumping anything more than a few years into a single view as 'long ago'. Alan Hodgkinson once observed a pupil asking, 'If Cleopatra had not been bitten by an asp would she still be alive today?'
- Problems with dating, especially BCE and CE and the mathematical dimension of time
- The past is seen as a series of stories and key events joined up like a list rather than an account of overlapping and interacting strands
- Change and progress are seen as interchangeable
- Tunnel vision and atomisation – information is seen in isolation and links between information are largely non-existent

How can we address this confusion?

Much of this relates to a sense of period. One of the most tried and tested ways has been through timelines, but it is important that timelines are used and aren't just classroom decorations. So, for example, timelines should indicate not just the order of things but how long the things lasted. It may not be necessary to depict actual dates but an idea of 'duration' is important and questions can be targeted on relative duration.

Many pupils muddle aspects of different societies or periods – especially features that were not especially distinctive. Some activities to eliminate such confusion include:

1. Use every opportunity to make links and connections so that pupils spot similarities, differences and links across time, place and theme rather than see history as formed of blocks without seeing links. For example, you could use overlapping timelines/three layers, such as local, national/world; thematic/development studies linking across time, for example, children, women, leisure or jobs with questions about change, similarity and difference.

2. At the beginning of a topic, make sure that pupils know what went before the period being studied, and try to make some links; try to get them to understand that period labels, such as 'Roman', did not mean that people existed outside this period, both before and after. Use timelines to show that things happened before and continued after the period they are studying. Can pupils think of some examples from their own lives where some things have changed but other things have stayed the same? Can they think of some period labels that describe their own lives, such as the age of the internet?
3. At the end of a topic, summarise what is most important. What we are seeking is some kind of synoptic grasp, what is significant and stands out. It is worth spending time at the end of a topic such as Ancient Egypt thinking about what they think were the two or three most important things that happened at that time. Do they think the most interesting things are also the most important?
4. Keep reinforcing important words in their vocabulary – change, continuity, progress, development. Keep asking questions about progress – when things changed, was everyone happy? Would some people have been upset? Can they think of changes in their lives that they think are 'progress' but other things that they do not feel the same way about? Now, can they think of things like that in history?

Confusion 2: Pupils not knowing enough so their contextual knowledge and understanding of terminology results in simplistic and naive history

What are some of the characteristics of this confusion?

- Stereotypical views, such as of old age, other races, women, countries and groups
- Hollywood and other depictions of things like castles, palaces, nobles, battles
- An inability to see the typicality of particular issues, situations, events and people
- Real difficulty telling the differences between small details and the most important aspects – everything is largely equal
- Pupils can answer individual questions but find it difficult to apply concepts to different contexts
- Poor general knowledge about place/geography, events, politics, culture, economics
- Poor recall, frequently forgetting what they have covered in individual lessons

How can we address this confusion?

Obviously, the main way is for pupils to experience the range of content, perspectives and dimensions to build up a wider database of knowledge. However, this can still cause confusion if treated in isolation. Some activities to eliminate some confusions include:

1. Show two parallel depictions, for example a theme park and an archaeological image or a *Horrible History* section and a set of written sources about a theme. Ask pupils to spot differences and explain why they might differ.
2. Constantly reinforce understanding by recall tests – not just about the immediate topic but previously covered ones. Every couple of weeks set a 15-question test with 10 devised by the teacher and 5 devised by pupils. Every now and again the test can involve a theme, for example, list 10 monarchs covered or 10 facts about buildings.
3. When asking a question, ask the pupils whether they remember a similar situation in another area they have covered, such as another battle won against the odds, another way in which children were badly treated, another key invention that changed lives. Alternatively, can they think of something they have covered which was very different in terms of situation or outcome?
4. Make sure that, when covering a topic, some time is devoted to the wider context including terminology. Ask pupils to find places on the map. What other places exist in the area? What exactly is a peasant or nobleman? What do we mean by government/ how did people rule themselves? How did people earn a living in this place at this time? Where does this appear on the timeline?

5. Above all, challenge stereotypes by referring to different historical examples of particular situations, for example make sure that there is a balanced depiction of racial, religious and cultural groups. The same applies to women – balance depiction of women as victims of oppression with examples of achievement and leadership.

Confusion 3: Why things happened and turned out as they did, including the role human beings played in making things happen

What are some of the characteristics of this confusion?

- People in the past seen as amusing, brutal and inferior compared with today
- A lack of respect and care for people in the past
- Past people and situations are seen as two-dimensional, and seen without complexity or inconsistency, for example, not understanding that feelings and attitudes in individuals change and vary
- Seeing a sense of the inevitable in human action – things just happen without reason. People did not really have choices
- Either things happen for one reason or lead to one result or if more than one is recognised, they have equal importance
- Failure to recognise the perspectives of people in their situations – for example, not seeing that we might see events clearly but that people at the time found them confusing and unintelligible
- Unreal grasp of horrors and problems, for example 'people did not die so badly in those days' after viewing actors get up after a death scene re-enactment

How can we address this confusion?

1. Ask pupils what is likely to happen to them or their community tomorrow or next week or next year. When they admit that they do not know for certain, try to get them to understand that people in the past did not know how things would turn out when they did things. Introduce the word 'hindsight' and explain what it means. Ask them to think about what might have surprised different people in the past and what they might have expected. Why were some things unexpected?
2. Regularly ask the question when studying almost any history topic: 'Why should we care?'.
3. Make sure that topics do not just deal with brutality, bloodshed and cruelty but that some attempt is made to balance things with positive aspects such as people battling against the odds, acts of kindness and the achievements of people and society.
4. Provide a list of causes (perhaps on cards) and ask the pupils which, if any, helped bring about some action or outcome. Alternatively, provide one cause and ask them to come up with other causes. Pupils can share ideas about which reasons were most important and whether there were links between causes, for example, did some things happen only because of other things happening?

Confusion 4: Not really grasping how sources can be used properly

What are some of the characteristics of this confusion?

- Sources are accepted at face value and trusted immediately. If any judgement is made about how reliable information is, the criteria are very simple such as 'The author is from a reliable profession/authority such as a teacher, book or monk so must be reliable' or 'It's accepted by the majority so is automatically alright'. Any source will do if it provides information.
- Alternatively, adopting a formulaic, defeatist attitude towards source material, such as, 'No one is alive today to prove it', or seeing all sources as characterised by bias, lies, misunderstanding or dogmatism. Because of the deficiencies, pupils believe that the information in the sources cannot be used at all.
- Pupils don't really know what many past sources looked like because they have not seen them and perhaps only view them in teacher-simplified versions such as brief extracts or worksheets. Pupils thus think that little effort is involved getting information from a historical source.

- Sources are seen as not suitable to be used to make deductions or inferences. The source only gives us the obvious surface information. If it does not provide obvious information, we cannot use it for anything else.

How can we address this confusion?

1. Make sure that pupils understand what an inference is. See how many inferences pupils can come up with. Get other pupils to agree or disagree with the inferences being made.
2. Ask pupils to imagine producing a source such as a painting a picture or producing a written document or devising a cartoon or even a caption. Why might you do it? How would you do it? What might you do to it if you wanted to show X or emphasise Y? If you wanted to mislead someone, what could you do? This sort of activity should be anchored in the historical context and not done context free.
3. How can a source be checked? Lead pupils to look at more than one source so that one can be cross-referenced against another. Pupils should gradually acquire a greater awareness of various types of resource that might be used for different enquiries. This can lead to comparing more than one source in terms of their usefulness and reliability for a specific question.
4. Show pupils 'real' documents or at least facsimiles of sources. One of the confusions pupils often have is the belief that sources are short extracts or provide exactly what is needed to answer a question rather than documents that have to be searched carefully to yield what might be partial and distorted evidence.

Confusion 5: There can be several ways of looking at things in history (interpretations)

Pupils often find interpretations or different representations confusing or distracting. Yet handling differing interpretations is a fundamental feature of history and it will be vital to their study of history at secondary school (and for some, beyond). The challenge for teachers is to get pupils interested enough to want to consider different ways in which things can be viewed.

What are some of the characteristics of this confusion?

- Seeing different views as meaning that someone is wrong. There can only be one correct version of things – the past is the past.
- A desire for simple 'right' answers and a dislike of uncertainty. Pupils are not interested in differing viewpoints. They often get in the way of a good story.
- Seeing a contemporary source as incontrovertible proof. ('We can know the real truth if someone was there')
- Inability to distinguish between facts, opinions and judgements

How can we address this confusion?

1. Arrange for an event to happen in the school classroom or playground without warning. Then ask the pupils to give their account of what they witnessed. Compare the views and ask the pupils why they are not all identical (hopefully they aren't). Some of the differences are likely to be related to accuracy but there should also be other differences such as what they thought was important or where they were located.
2. Provide a brief account of an historical event. Pupils have to distinguish what is a definite concrete piece of information or what is an opinion or judgement. Alternatively, ask them to devise an account that includes some fact and some opinion.
3. Provide a narrative of a historical story or biography of a key character. Leave out one key part. Pupils individually have to fill in that section. How and why are there different answers in that section?
4. When a major topic is finished, ask pupils to select six objects that they think best exemplify the topic. Pupils discuss with others why they have chosen the object they have to represent that topic.

Confusion 6: Pupils not fully understanding what teachers are asking of them

What are some of the characteristics of this confusion?

This is not quite the same as the other misconceptions but it is a confusion nevertheless. We use many different command words or instructions in history teaching. Although they are not unique to history, there are a number of types of questions that we expect pupils to handle, but they may not be clear about what these questions mean. Not all these questions will be asked in all books, but in addition to the usual what, where, when questions, pupils could meet instructions such as:

1. Account for
2. Argue
3. Comment on
4. Compare
5. Consider
6. Criticise
7. Debate
8. Define
9. Describe
10. Devise
11. Discuss
12. Distinguish
13. Examine
14. Explain how/why/what/whether
15. Give an account
16. How reliable
17. How similar/different
18. How useful
19. Illustrate
20. Investigate
21. Justify/prove
22. List
23. Outline
24. Recall
25. Recount
26. Review
27. Summarise
28. To what extent/how far?

How can we address this confusion?

1. Although this may take time and reinforcement, the straightforward way is to ensure that pupils are regularly asked to complete tasks using such command words and instructions. Teachers can share pupils' work and ask whether individual pieces of work have 'answered what was being asked for'.
2. Make sure that pupils do not have unreal expectations about what they have to do – get them in habits such as ensuring that when asked why something happened, it is not usually enough to select just one reason (especially the first that comes into their head) but that several are expected. Pupils need to

understand that surface answers are rarely good enough in history. They should be encouraged to be tentative in their answers recognising that there can be both uncertainty and alternatives.

3. Do not accept simple copying from a book or extensive plagiarism. In history, pupils need to be encouraged to come up with possible answers using their own ideas and then to provide some historical fact or piece of evidence to 'prove' it. Pupils can share thoughts on which pupils have used good evidence to 'prove' the point they are trying to make.
4. Get pupils to ask their own questions before looking at a topic and then discussing what makes a good question to ask – not just a series of 'what' questions.

Conclusion

An interest in history may come naturally but an understanding may be that much more difficult to achieve. Good teachers develop the knowledge, skills and understandings in a coherent and progressive way. These need constant reinforcement. While there can be much debate about what a real historical understanding is, there is surely no argument that suggests that we should just ignore these obvious misconceptions. The modern world indicates the dangers of leaders pontificating based on a distorted and confused historical understanding.

A longer version of the article upon which this section was based, by Tim Lomas, with lots of practical examples of activities to counter such confusions, first appeared in 'Primary History,' the Primary members' journal of the Historical Association (www.history.org.uk.)

What does it mean to get better at history?

Getting better at history means:

- **wider, more detailed and chronologically secure knowledge**

As pupils get older, they develop a more detailed knowledge of history, and how it fits together. For example, they might be able to compare Stone Age Britain with a stone-age society like the Maya, having studied both. They ought to know that the Romans came before the Anglo-Saxons, for example, but also be able to build on their existing knowledge. They might, for example, be able to use their knowledge of pyramids in Ancient Egypt to decide what questions they want to ask about pyramids in Maya life.

- **sharper methods of enquiry and communication**

As they get older, pupils ought to be able to be more critical of evidence they find, asking questions such as, 'Why does this person say that? Do I trust them? Another person says something different – how do I decide which one to believe?' Answers might be much less black and white, with nuances that reflect the differences in the evidence, or in historians' views.

- **deeper understanding of more complex issues and of abstract ideas**

History is complicated and, as they get more confident, pupils should both understand this – people react in different ways in the same situation – and make use of it in their work. There is usually no simple answer to historical problems, and an understanding of that is a sign of increasing historical maturity.

- **making greater use of history's concepts and skills**

History is not just about content, it is also a process of study. As pupils get better at history, they ought to move away from an emphasis on content to an increasing emphasis on process – **why** something happened rather than **what** happened, for example.

- **greater independence in applying all these qualities**

Finally, pupils ought increasingly to be able to ask their own questions of history, decide how to find evidence, and how to present their conclusions; in other words, they need to become more self-reliant in deciding how they investigate topics.

Where to find out more

General support for teaching and learning history:

- The Historical Association (**www.history.org.uk**) is a subject association for history teachers. They publish a journal, *Primary History,* three times a year. Their website has Schemes of Work, articles and podcasts supporting all areas of primary history.

- Museums like the British Museum (**www.britishmuseum.org**) (in London) have a lot of free online materials – images and text – aimed at helping teachers.

- BBC History website (**www.bbc.co.uk/history**) contains lots of detailed briefing notes to help teachers understand key topics.

- BBC Bitesize website (**www.bbc.com/bitesize**) has lots of useful links to materials children can use.

- Firms like TTS (**www.tts-group.co.uk/**) sell copies of artefacts that help bring history to life. There is nothing quite like holding a 5000-year-old stone axe to bring history alive. Replicas are the next best thing.

Teaching history to pupils aged 5–7

Changes Within Living Memory

Overview of Pupil Book contents

Unit	Content
1	Let's go shopping! – learning about the history of shopping for food, including the first supermarket in 1951, the introduction of fridges, freezers and microwaves, what people were buying in the 1960s and 1970s, and how people paid for their shopping. Comparing how people shopped for food in the past to how we shop for food today.
2	Time for play – learning about the history of children's toys. Comparing historic toys and games to modern toys and games, discussing similarities and differences.
3	Washday – learning about the history of washing clothes, including laundrettes and washing machines, what happened on wash day, and how people wash clothes today.
4	Granny's got a tablet! – learning about the history of communication, including computers and the internet, phones, and the postal system.
5	A new coat – exploring how people bought coats in the past and comparing this to how people buy them today.
6	Going to school – learning about the history of schools, including what the outside and inside of schools looked like and what children learned, and making comparisons to modern school systems.
7	Are we nearly there yet? – learning about the history of going on holiday, including seaside holidays in Britain, holiday camps, theme parks and camping.
8	Feeling poorly … – exploring what people did when they felt ill in the past and comparing to what people do today. Learning about the introduction of the NHS, diseases of the past and present, and prevention of diseases and treatments for illnesses today.

Timeline: Changes Within Living Memories

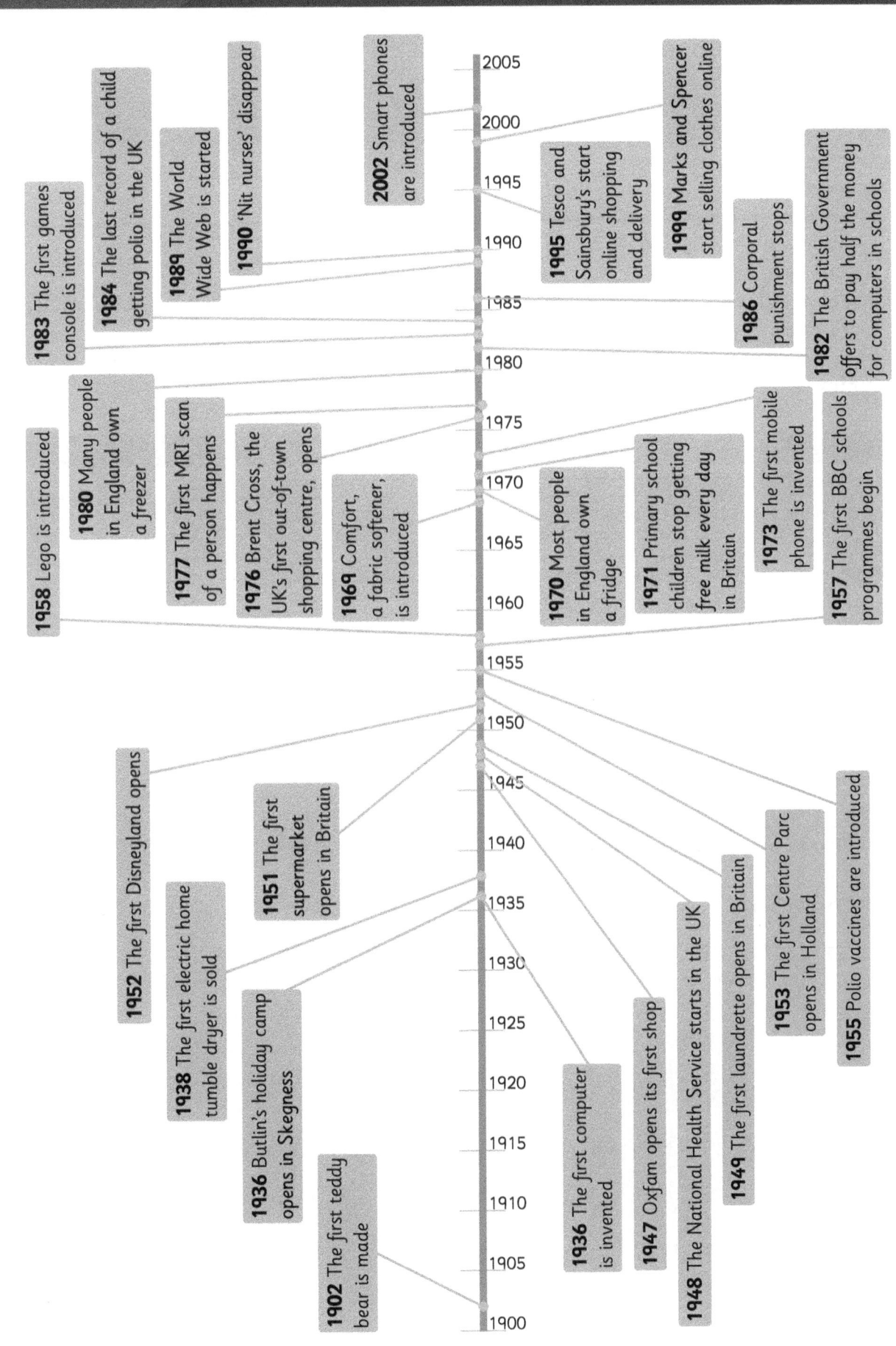

- **1902** The first teddy bear is made
- **1936** The first computer is invented
- **1936** Butlin's holiday camp opens in Skegness
- **1938** The first electric home tumble dryer is sold
- **1947** Oxfam opens its first shop
- **1948** The National Health Service starts in the UK
- **1949** The first laundrette opens in Britain
- **1951** The first supermarket opens in Britain
- **1952** The first Disneyland opens
- **1953** The first Centre Parc opens in Holland
- **1955** Polio vaccines are introduced
- **1957** The first BBC schools programmes begin
- **1958** Lego is introduced
- **1969** Comfort, a fabric softener, is introduced
- **1970** Most people in England own a fridge
- **1971** Primary school children stop getting free milk every day in Britain
- **1973** The first mobile phone is invented
- **1976** Brent Cross, the UK's first out-of-town shopping centre, opens
- **1977** The first MRI scan of a person happens
- **1980** Many people in England own a freezer
- **1982** The British Government offers to pay half the money for computers in schools
- **1983** The first games console is introduced
- **1984** The last record of a child getting polio in the UK
- **1986** Corporal punishment stops
- **1989** The World Wide Web is started
- **1990** 'Nit nurses' disappear
- **1995** Tesco and Sainsbury's start online shopping and delivery
- **1999** Marks and Spencer start selling clothes online
- **2002** Smart phones are introduced

HarperCollins*Publishers* 2019

Knowledge organiser and skills grid

Knowledge organiser

Some suggested steps for helping pupils to produce a simple knowledge organiser:
- Focus on one aspect.
- Describe how this aspect was then.
- Describe how it is now.
- Why do you think it changed? (new materials? new technology?)
- What is it different between then and now?
- What is it the same between then and now?
- What evidence did we use to find out about this? (for example photographs/pictures, artefacts/objects, oral history, documents – letters, diaries and so on).

Skills grid

Activity	History skills targeted
Placing the person/changes on the class timeline	Chronological Understanding
Using appropriate vocabulary relating to the passage of time	Chronological Understanding
Examining and discussing evidence (sources of information) for example an artefact/object (Spinning Top – examining artefacts)	Historical Enquiry
Interviewing a person remembering their own experiences (Oral History) or an expert on that topic	Historical Enquiry
Identify same/different (for example School comparison chart or Picture sort – wash day)	Knowledge and Understanding
Asking and answering questions	Knowledge and Understanding
Be able to recognise what is evidence and sources of information	Knowledge and Understanding and Historical Enquiry
Giving simple opinions	Knowledge and Understanding and Historical Interpretation

Teaching about changes within living memory to pupils aged 5–7

This book explores living memories – the remembrances of people who are still alive. This can be a very powerful learning experience for younger children who may only have been presented with other people's interpretations of the past; interviewing a real person about their own experiences, known as 'Oral History' could be a lesson they will always remember. Artefacts can also be a useful way of introducing children to the past through primary sources. Being able to handle older objects appeals to young children's senses and that kinaesthetic experience can be engaging and intriguing for them.

Artefacts

As you read the different sections, encourage pupils to think about what this aspect of their lives is like now and how it is different to the experiences described in the book. Using artefacts for pupils to handle helps to bring the past alive for them – and examples of irons, clothes, toys and other objects from the more recent past will be easier to track down than artefacts from a long time ago. Ask pupils to ask their families if they have examples in cupboards at home – it's amazing what will turn up! One school I work with created a permanent museum in one classroom from all the artefacts that members of their local community contributed. You may not get this much but setting up a class museum will encourage pupils to return to the objects for closer observation time and again, helping them to process the information and explore for themselves.

As you explore and discuss individual artefacts, encourage pupils to think about:

- What is it made of? How do you know? Is it made from a natural substance? Is it made from different substances?
- Why do you think those materials were chosen? Has it been repaired?
- Who cleans it? What do they use? Is it worn?
- What does it look/feel/sound/smell like? What colour/shape/size is it?
- How was it made? – machine/hand/mould/in pieces/ at once or over time/one person or several? Is it complete? Has it been altered or adapted? Have bits been taken away or added?
- What was it made for? How has it been used? Has its use changed?
- Is it well designed? Is it efficient? Were the best materials chosen?
- How is it decorated? Why is it decorated? Is it pleasing to look at? Why?
- What is the object worth? To you? To its owner? To a bank?

You can use Resource sheet: Time for play – Artefact observation as support.

Oral History

Organising an oral history interview takes a little time but is so rewarding for your pupils. Your pupils' families, friends and the local community can become much more involved in a project based around oral history. Here are some suggestions of things you could focus on:

- Local history, for example a street, village or school community
- Single issue themes – history of a factory, building or house, for example the school, or other significant building
- Single event – Coronation Day, Silver Jubilee but could also be something much more local like a flood or the opening of a significant building
- Subject areas – any of the topics covered in this book would make a good basis for a project but also tea time, religious festivals and so on
- Individual life event – evacuees, emigrating and so on
- Leisure and sport – theatre, cinema, being on a local sports team
- Family history – you could potentially have four or five generations of a family alive – unlikely to continue for long as women in some parts of the world are having babies much later in life
- Culture – helping the children to explore different cultures and traditions

In order to find someone suitable, you may need to ask friends and family for recommendations or contact a local history or museum. Be aware that not everyone can cope with a class of children asking questions, no matter how well behaved! You might find it helpful to arrange for the visitor to have lunch with the children before joining their class so they are more comfortable talking to them prior to the interview. It is better to approach the person yourself rather than by letter or email so you can explain exactly what you are looking for and answer any questions there and then.

In order to prepare for the interview, do some research with your pupils. Examine artefacts, books and images and support the children to prepare a list of questions. Do not be too rigid, encourage them to use the list as a memory prompt. It is also useful to help the pupils understand that how they phrase the question is really important; they need to use open questions which allow the interviewee to give detailed answers – not questions which you can answer with yes or no. Using 'Tell me about …', or what, why, how and describe encourages and allows the interviewee to give fuller answers and this is a useful skill for pupils to develop. Encourage pupils to ask questions to set the context, time, place and so on also. Ask the person to bring any relevant photos and artefacts with them as this can help them to remember in more detail. It is good manners to send thank you letters from the pupils afterwards and you might find it useful to tape or video the interview – but always check for permission.

Good luck!

Resource sheet: Time for play – Artefact observation

What does it look like?
What is made of?
How do you think it was played with?
When was it used?

✂--

Use a real artefact/object – this is important to give pupils a better idea of the size, weight and so on. For example, you may show a spinning top like the one here:

Consider:

What does it look like?

What colour is it? (Bright colours to make it attractive) What designs are on it? (A child with toys, a boy fishing, a motorcycle) Why is the handle not decorated? (Because any decoration would rub off)

What is made of?

Does it use more than one material? (Metal and wood – wood is more comfortable for the pushing action) Do we still use these materials for toys now? (Sometimes but more plastics are used) Was it is a good choice? (It has lasted well) Does it work well for this toy? (It still works) Is it heavy or light? (Compare it to a modern toy)

How do you think it was played with?

Who do you think might have played with it? Was it designed for a boy or a girl or either? (Both boys and girls played with these) What did you have to do to make it work? (Push up and down on the handle to make it spin. It needs to be on a flat surface) Do we have anything like this now? (for example fidget spinners)

When was it used?

How old do you think this is? (Spinning tops have been around for a very long time – one was found in Iraq from 1300 BCE – there was even one in Tutankhamun's tomb! This one is probably from around 1950) Do your toys look like this one? (They might have similar characters on their toys/games) What is different? What is the same? (Colours/materials/design)

HarperCollins*Publishers* 2019

Resource sheet: Wash day – Picture sort

Sort the pictures into the diagram.

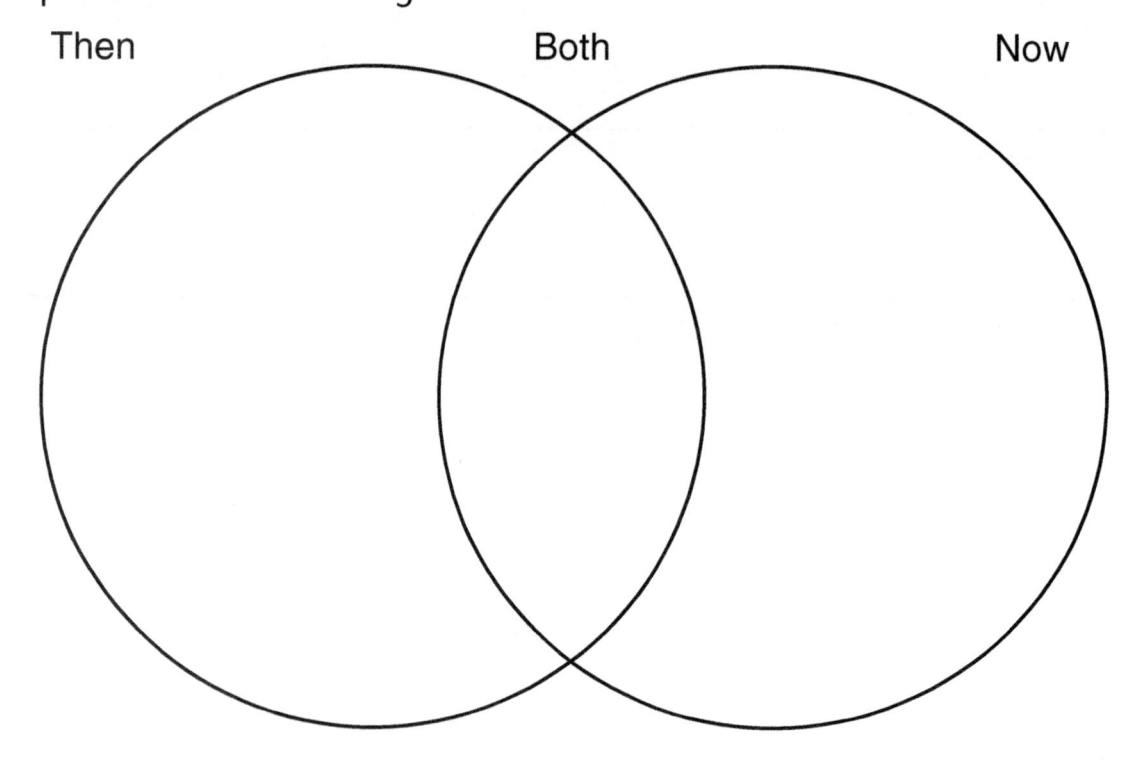

Then　　　　　　　　　Both　　　　　　　　　Now

✂ ---

Cut out the pictures below and ask pupils to sort them into 'then' and 'now'. The pictures could be stuck into the pupils' books, sorted onto a Venn diagram.

30　　　　　　　　　　　　　　　　　　　　　　　HarperCollins*Publishers* 2019

Resource sheet: Going to school – School comparison chart

	What I do at school	**When my parents were at school**	**When my grandparents were at school**
What are/were the desks like?			
What kinds of toys or equipment do/did you use?			
What subjects do/did you learn?			
What is/was the school dinner like?			
What do/did you do at playtime?			
What are/were the punishments if you did something wrong?			
How do/did you get to school?			

✂ ---

Ask pupils to collect information from their parents and grandparents (or family friends of a similar age) to complete a chart like this one. You could leave some blank rows for them to add their own questions.

If you have a visitor to the classroom talking about their school days, this table could be adapted. Something similar could also be used for other aspects of life in the past compared to today.

Pupil Book model answers

What to look for to ensure progression and understanding

Chronological understanding

In history, there is rarely a 'right' or 'wrong' answer – as a teacher you are encouraging the class to develop their understanding of how we know about the past, and the job of a historian/archaeologist. In order to develop pupils' knowledge and understanding, you need to be asking lots of questions which help pupils to think about the sources of information you are using; the sources. Who wrote this? When was it written? How did they know this? Why was it recorded? Where was it written? Compare sources – What is the same? What is different? What has been left out? Why?

Adding information to the class timeline and encouraging them to use appropriate vocabulary (before, after, then, now, decade and so on) and ordering events in the life of an interviewee will help your pupils to begin to have an appreciation of what happened when – this will not be completely developed at this stage but we need to support and encourage this from the start.

Historical enquiry

Learning about changes and events within living memory gives pupils the ideal opportunity to do some oral history such as interviewing a real person who remembers either a specific event or can talk about the changes in aspects of daily life and what is the same and what is different. Examining and discussing this evidence can be a very powerful experience for pupils as they realise they are acting like real historians. Exploring objects and photographs of simple implements from people's daily lives helps pupils to develop observational and analytical skills at a basic level but these are firm foundations for their future study.

Knowledge and understanding

Using oral history and objects and photographs all help pupils to identify similarities and differences and these can help your class to appreciate some of the changes in national lives as well as locally. Using the School comparison chart and the Picture sort: Washday activities encourages pupils to talk about the common changes and what has stayed the same.

In order to ensure that your pupils' understanding is secure, encourage them to ask their own questions as well as answer your questions. Encouraging them to use When? Who? Why? Where? How? as question starters will help to scaffold this important skill. Supporting your class in developing empathy is also an important aspect and interviewing a real person will support this.

Historical interpretation

Children of this age should be beginning to recognise evidence and sources and offer simple opinions – encourage them to justify these by asking why they think that and what evidence do they have to support this, when completing the School comparison chart for example. Annotating images or simple documents also supports children to consider exactly what this evidence is showing them.

Above all have fun with your pupils – your enthusiasm and encouragement are the key things in developing a love for history.

Events Beyond Living Memory

Overview of Pupil Book contents

Unit	Content
1	Mount Vesuvius and Pompeii – learning about the eruption of Mount Vesuvius including an eye-witness account, and discussing the consequences of the eruption for the people in Pompeii. Linking to modern volcano eruption. Exploring what life in Pompeii was like before and after the eruption of Mount Vesuvius. Discussing how we know what happened.
2	Discovering Angkor Wat – learning about Henri Mouhot and his four journeys into the jungles of Laos, Cambodia and Thailand. Exploring what life was like in Angkor, and what we have learned over time about Angkor and the Khmer people.
3	Sailing around the world – learning about Ferdinand Magellan's voyage around the world. Exploring what life was like in the Middle Ages, and what happened after Magellan's voyage.
4	The Great Fire of London – learning about the Great Fire of London, including how it started, how it spread and how it was fought. Exploring what life was like in London in 1966, and what happened after the fire.
5	HMS *Birkenhead*: Women and children first! – learning about HMS *Birkenhead*'s final journey and the sinking of the ship. Exploring what life was like in Victorian times and why people travelled. Discussing the lasting consequences of the sinking of HMS *Birkenhead* – women and children first.
6	The Crystal Palace – learning about the Great Exhibition in the Crystal Palace. Exploring what life was like in Britain in 1851, and discussing the impact of the Exhibition.
7	Finding Tutankhamun's tomb – learning about Howard Carter and Lord Caernarvon's discovery of Tutankhamun's tomb. Exploring what life was like in Ancient Egypt, and how the discovery of the tomb has helped us learn more about this period and how the Ancient Egyptians might have lived.
8	Amy Johnson flies to Australia – learning about Amy Johnson's flight to Australia. Exploring what life was like in the 1920s, including how people travelled and what they thought about Amy Johnson. Discussing what happened in Amy's life after her flight to Australia.

Timeline: Events Beyond Living Memory

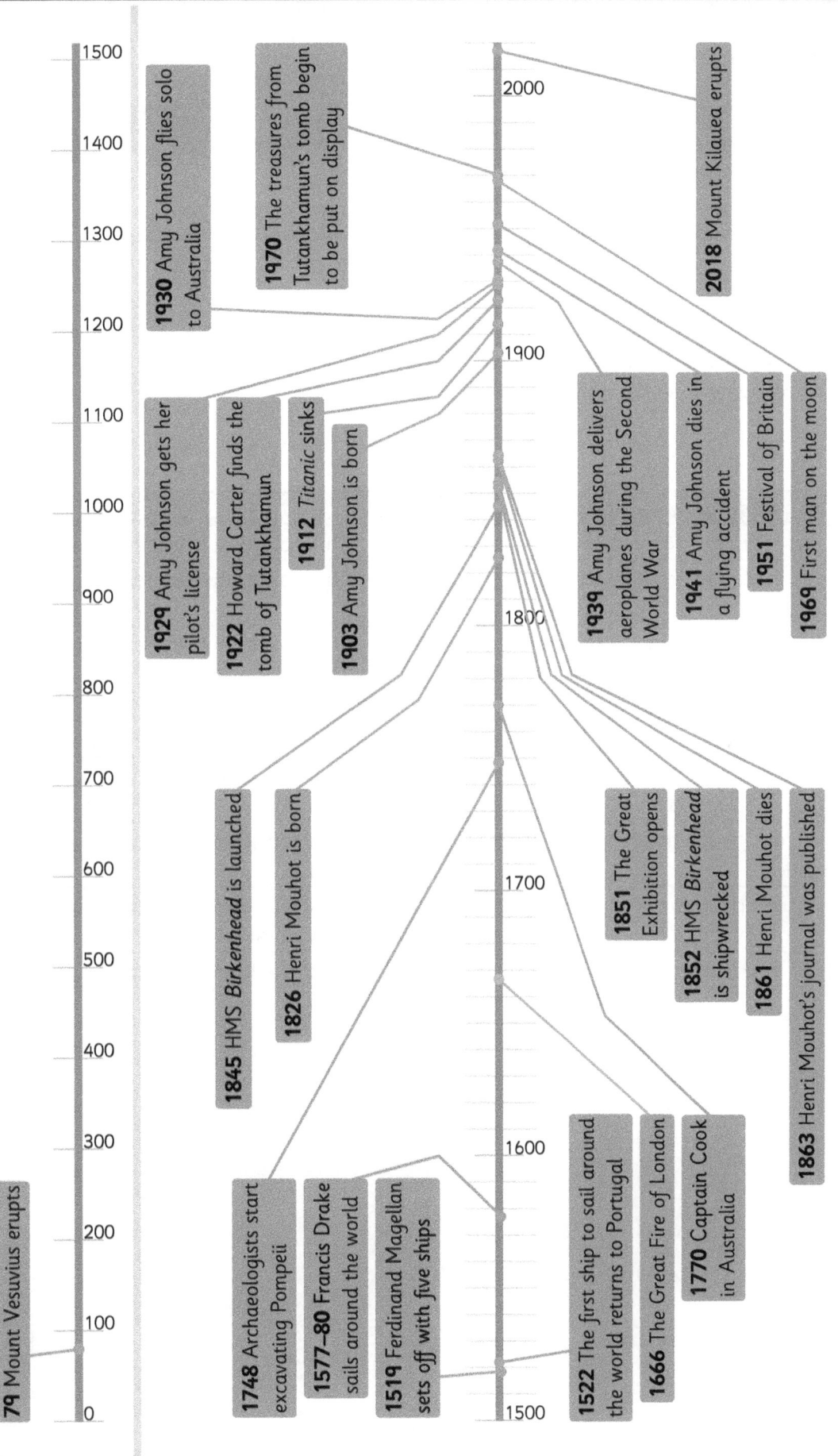

- 79 Mount Vesuvius erupts
- 1519 Ferdinand Magellan sets off with five ships
- 1522 The first ship to sail around the world returns to Portugal
- 1577–80 Francis Drake sails around the world
- 1666 The Great Fire of London
- 1748 Archaeologists start excavating Pompeii
- 1770 Captain Cook in Australia
- 1826 Henri Mouhot is born
- 1845 HMS Birkenhead is launched
- 1851 The Great Exhibition opens
- 1852 HMS Birkenhead is shipwrecked
- 1861 Henri Mouhot dies
- 1863 Henri Mouhot's journal was published
- 1903 Amy Johnson is born
- 1912 Titanic sinks
- 1922 Howard Carter finds the tomb of Tutankhamun
- 1929 Amy Johnson gets her pilot's license
- 1930 Amy Johnson flies solo to Australia
- 1939 Amy Johnson delivers aeroplanes during the Second World War
- 1941 Amy Johnson dies in a flying accident
- 1951 Festival of Britain
- 1969 First man on the moon
- 1970 The treasures from Tutankhamun's tomb begin to be put on display
- 2018 Mount Kilauea erupts

HarperCollins*Publishers* 2019

Knowledge organiser and skills grid

Knowledge organiser

Some suggested steps for helping pupils to produce a simple knowledge organiser:
- Focus on one event.
- What happened that was important or memorable?
- Where did the event take place?
- When did the event take place?
- What was going on at that time?
- How did it change what was happening at the time?
- What evidence did we use to find out about them? (for example visual images, documents – letters, diaries, maps and so on, artefacts/objects and so on)
- How do we remember this event? How should we remember it?

Skills grid

Activity	History skills targeted
Placing the event on the class timeline	Chronological Understanding
Using appropriate vocabulary relating to the passage of time	Chronological Understanding
Ordering statements about an event into chronological order (for example Great Fire of London ordering statements activity)	Chronological Understanding
Asking and answering questions	Knowledge and Understanding
Completing Think bubbles activities (for example HMS *Birkenhead* activity)	Knowledge and Understanding and Developing Empathy
Be able to recognise what is evidence and sources of information	Knowledge and Understanding and Historical Enquiry
Giving simple opinions	Knowledge and Understanding and Historical Interpretation
Annotating an image	Historical Interpretation

Teaching about events beyond living memory to pupils aged 5–7

Everyone will have different ideas about what should be included in a list of these significant events! We have chosen a range of different events from around the world to demonstrate the diversity in what you can choose to teach your pupils. We do hope you are inspired to find out more and maybe introduce some new world events into your classroom!

Significance

Pupils should be taught how to appreciate 'significance'. Ian Dawson gives an excellent working definition of what constitutes a significant individual, so we have adapted that to consider significant events:

An event is significant if it:

- changed events at the time (for example the first female flight, the Great Fire of London)
- improved lots of people's lives – or made them worse (for example Crystal Palace, Pompeii, HMS *Birkenhead*)
- changed people's ideas (for example Crystal Palace, discovering the Angkor Wat, sailing around the world, finding Tutankhamun's tomb)
- had a long-lasting impact on their country or the world (for example discovering Angkor Wat and Tutankhamun's tomb, first female flight, Pompeii)
- had been a really good, or a very bad example to other people of how to live or behave (the first female flight, HMS *Birkenhead*, sailing around the world).

How do we know what happened?

Pupils need to appreciate that we know about these events due to evidence, and that evidence can be a range of different things. It could be diaries or writings/log books (for example Henri Mouhot's writings, Samuel Pepys' diaries or Ferdinand Magellan's ship log), it could be a historic site which is being excavated (for example Angkor Wat, Tutankhamun's tomb or Pompeii), it could be paintings or pictures (for example the Great Fire of London or HMS *Birkenhead*) and it could be newspaper articles (for example about the Great Exhibition or Amy Johnson's flight). Maps are also a very useful source of information and explanation in many of these events; understanding how much of London was burned down during the Great Fire of London, showing just how remote Angkor Wat is and how far Magellan's voyage turned out to be.

Bias and eye-witnesses

Eye witness accounts would seem to be the best kind of evidence you could find; however, we do need to encourage children to be critical and look carefully for evidence of bias. Who was the intended audience and what was the purpose of the writing? For example, Henri Mouhot was recording mainly for himself, whereas Ferdinand Magellan was paid by the King of Spain so it is reasonable to assume that he might want to see the ships' logs. It would not, therefore, be in Magellan's interests to record when things went a little awry!

HarperCollins*Publishers* 2019

What archaeologists do, and how is their job changing

It is important for pupils to understand the job of a historian, and most especially an archaeologist, so they can begin to appreciate the process that takes place to interpret evidence and make educated guesses about what has happened. The story of Henri Mouhot and his 'wrong' ideas is an interesting one to share with pupils, to show that even intelligent people do not always have enough knowledge or evidence to make the correct assumptions and theories.

The job of archaeologists is changing all the time as new technologies are introduced. These technologies can illuminate aspects which have been impossible to work out previously; for example, the DNA and bone testing which has more recently been used on Tutankhamun's skeleton has given archaeologists information about his likely parentage and the diseases and conditions he may have suffered from.

The new radar system called lidar has recently been used to uncover vast tracts of ruins around Angkor Wat which archaeologists were not aware of as they had been lost deep in the jungle. Lidar creates detailed 3D images of the land without needing to dig so that ancient waterways, streets and other buildings can be uncovered.

Camera drones can soar above sites taking photographs and video footage, which may show changes in the growth of vegetation that indicate disturbances in the soil that could be evidence of human activity. Sophisticated software can then be used to create 3D models of the sites; virtual replicas that are geographically accurate representations which can then be examined in detail from the safety of an office, without wasting time and money excavating areas that yield little evidence.

Muon tomography is used by archaeologists to visualise the space inside structures they cannot get into, for example Egyptian pyramids or underground tombs, without doing any damage to the original building. A technique called muon scattering tomography uses these elementary particles generated by natural and artificial cosmic rays. Muons can penetrate deep into rocks such as limestone and granite which are particularly challenging to excavate.

Timelines and chronology

Children of this age need to experience a variety of different timelines to encourage their building understanding of chronology. Using a variety of scales helps pupils to grapple with the concept of chronological understanding; for example, the Great Fire of London is measured in days, whereas the Khmer civilisation goes back thousands of years. Many young children will not really have a good understanding of how long ago this was, but this does not mean we should avoid it – they will slowly build up this understanding through repeated exposure and discussions.

Resource sheet: Mount Vesuvius and Pompeii – Evaluating sources

	Evidence (which sources show this)
The people tried to run away.	
The lava ran down the mountain quickly setting fire to anything nearby.	
The eruption was very violent with pumice stones being thrown in the air.	
The thick clouds made it seem like night.	
People tried to escape in boats.	
People were killed by the heat and hot gases.	

Which source is most useful?

....

....

Which source is least useful?

....

....

Which source is the most reliable?

....

....

What else do the sources tell us?

....

....

What else would you like to find out?

....

....

HarperCollins*Publishers* 2019

Source 1:

Source 2:

Source 3:

Source 4:

Extract from a translated letter written by Pliny the Younger soon after to his friend describing what happened:

> "They debated whether to stay indoors or take their chance in the open, for the buildings were now shaking with violent shocks, and seemed to be swaying to and fro as if they were torn from their foundations. Outside, on the other hand, there was the danger of falling pumice stones, even though these were light and porous; however, after comparing the risks they chose the latter. In my uncle's case one reason outweighed the other, but for the others it was a choice of fears. As a protection against falling objects they put pillows on their heads tied down with cloths.
>
> Elsewhere there was daylight by this time, but they were still in darkness, blacker and denser than any ordinary night, which they relieved by lighting torches and various kinds of lamp. My uncle decided to go down to the shore and investigate on the spot the possibility of any escape by sea, but he found the waves still wild and dangerous. A sheet was spread on the ground for him to lie down, and he repeatedly asked for cold water to drink.
>
> Then the flames and smell of sulfur which gave warning of the approaching fire drove the others to take flight and roused him to stand up. He stood leaning on two slaves and then suddenly collapsed, I imagine because the dense, fumes choked his breathing by blocking his windpipe which was constitutionally weak and narrow and often inflamed. When daylight returned on the 26th – two days after the last day he had been seen – his body was found intact and uninjured, still fully clothed and looking more like sleep than death."
>
> 'The Destruction of Pompeii, 79 CE', EyeWitness to History, www.eyewitnesstohistory.com (1999).

Provide children with the above images and text extract so they can fill in the table and answer the questions at the bottom of the resource sheet.

HarperCollins*Publishers* 2019

Resource sheet: HMS *Birkenhead* – Think bubbles

✂---

Insert thought bubbles (or use post-it notes) onto a painting or photograph and encourage pupils to think about what that particular person will be feeling and thinking. This helps them to develop empathy with the people having these experiences.

This activity could be used with other events such as the Vesuvius eruption and building Crystal Palace or with individuals such as Amy Johnson or Howard Carter. Look for an understanding of how the person would be feeling as well as an understanding of what is happening.

Resource sheet: Mount Vesuvius and Pompeii – Sorting statements (True/False)

Mount Vesuvius was in France.
Only 15 people died.
Pompeii was a village of 200 people.
This happened in the Tudor era.
Most people were killed by the heat and hot gases.
Pompeii was covered completely by the lava, hiding any sign of the city.
There had been an earthquake 17 years before and people were rebuilding the city.
We know about what happened because there was an eye-witness who wrote down what he saw.
Archaeologists try to find out what happened in the past by digging up historical sites.

Examples of opinion statements you could add if required.

It was the worst eruption ever seen.
Pompeii shouldn't have been built so close to the volcano.
Archaeologists believe more than 1500 people died.

✂--

Pompeii and Mount Vesuvius

Split the class into small groups and give each group a copy of these statements. Pupils sort the statements into true/false. If you have a group of particularly able pupils, you could make some fact or opinion statements.
This activity could be used with most history topics.

Answers:

- ✗ Mount Vesuvius was in France.
- ✗ Only 15 people died.
- ✗ Pompeii was a village of 200 people.
- ✗ This happened in the Tudor era.
- ✓ Most people were killed by the heat and hot gases.
- ✓ Pompeii was covered completely by the lava, hiding any sign of the city.
- ✓ There had been an earthquake 17 years before and people were rebuilding the city.
- ✓ We know about what happened because there was an eye-witness who wrote down what he saw.
- ✓ Archaeologists try to find out what happened in the past by digging up historical sites.

HarperCollins Publishers 2019

Resource sheet: The Great Fire of London – Ordering statements

Many people had to flee their houses and shelter in stone buildings like churches.
King Charles II was the king at the time.
The summer of 1666 had been very hot.
The Great Fire of London started on 2 September in a baker's shop on Pudding Lane.
The fire burned for five days and then some of the houses were blown up to stop the fire spreading even further.
The wind helped to spread the fire and there was no rain.
We think the fire started because the oven fire was not 'damped down' and a spark jumped onto some kindling.
The King ordered that tents be put up so the homeless people had somewhere to stay.
The houses were made of wood and were built close together so the fire spread easily.
The Bakers was owned by Thomas Faryner.
Samuel Pepys wrote in his diary about the fire.
People all over the country collected money to help rebuild London.
The new buildings were made of stone and not built so close to each other.

✂--

Great Fire of London

Cut out or copy the statements above. Pupils put the statements in order to tell the story of what happened. You may decide to give fewer statements to less able pupils and more to more able pupils. This could be an individual activity or completed in small groups. As there is no single correct answer, pupils may find it useful to discuss their chosen order with classmates.

Pupil Book model answers

What to look for to ensure progression and understanding

Chronological understanding

In history there is rarely a 'right' or 'wrong' answer – as a teacher you are encouraging the class to develop their understanding of how we know about the past, and the job of a historian/archaeologist. In order to develop pupils' knowledge and understanding you need to be asking lots of questions which help pupils to think about the sources of information you are using. Who wrote this? When was it written? How did they know this? Why was it recorded? Where was it written? Compare sources – What is the same? What is different? What has been left out? Why?

Placing the event on the class timeline, encouraging them to use appropriate vocabulary (before, after, decade, century and so on) and ordering statements about an event (see The Great Fire of London – Ordering statements activity) will all help your pupils to begin to have an appreciation of what happened when – this will not be completely developed at this stage but we need to support and encourage this from the start of their studies.

Knowledge and understanding

In order to ensure that your pupils' understanding is secure, encourage them to ask their own questions as well as answer your questions. Encouraging them to use When? Who? Why? Where? How? as question starters will help to scaffold this important skill. Supporting your pupils in developing empathy is also an important aspect of this (see HMS *Birkenhead* – Think bubbles activity). Children of this age should be beginning to recognise evidence and sources and offer simple opinions – encourage them to justify these by asking why they think as they do and what evidence do they have to support this.

Historical interpretation

Children need to evaluate the usefulness of the sources they are using (see Mount Vesuvius and Pompeii – Evaluating sources activity). Consider the 3 Rs of Archives with your pupils:

Rich – how much detail or information does it give you?

Relevant – is the information useful to this activity?

Reliable – where has the information come from, was it produced at the time?

This is an important life skill which will be used in pupils' later education whenever they use the internet for research, and will enable them to approach news stories critically. Supporting your pupils to analyse sources – for example exploring the details in the HMS *Birkenhead* picture, using the Pompeii evaluating sources activity or using sorting cards (true/false or fact/opinion) all support children in developing their ability to interpret and interrogate sources.

Above all have fun with your pupils – your enthusiasm and encouragement are the key things in developing a love for history.

Significant Individuals

Overview of Pupil Book contents

Unit	Content
1	Fu Hao – learning about the discovery of Fu Hao's tomb. Exploring what life was like in China during the Shang dynasty, and what the discovery of the tomb has taught us about Fu Hao.
2	Ibn Battuta – learning about Ibn Battuta's travels to Mecca. Exploring what life was like in 600 CE, and the spread of Islam. Discussing the reliability of Ibn Battuta's accounts.
3	Henry VIII – learning about the life of Henry VIII, from when he became King, to his six marriages, to what happened after his divorce from Catherine of Aragon.
4	Shah Jahan – exploring who Shah Jahan was, what life was like in India in 1628, and the building of the Taj Mahal.
5	Martha Ricks – learning about the life of Martha Ricks, from being a slave in Tennessee, to her move to Liberia, to her trip to Britain to meet Queen Victoria.
6	Rosa Parks – learning about the abolition of slavery in the United States of America, the continuing separation of people because of the colour of their skin. Learning about the civil rights movement, with a focus on Rosa Park's bus boycott.
7	Agnodice and Elizabeth Garrett Anderson – learning about two historic female doctors and their lives.
8	Captain James Cook and Neil Armstrong – learning about two historic male voyagers, what they found out from their explorations, and the chronology of their lives.

Timeline: Significant Individuals

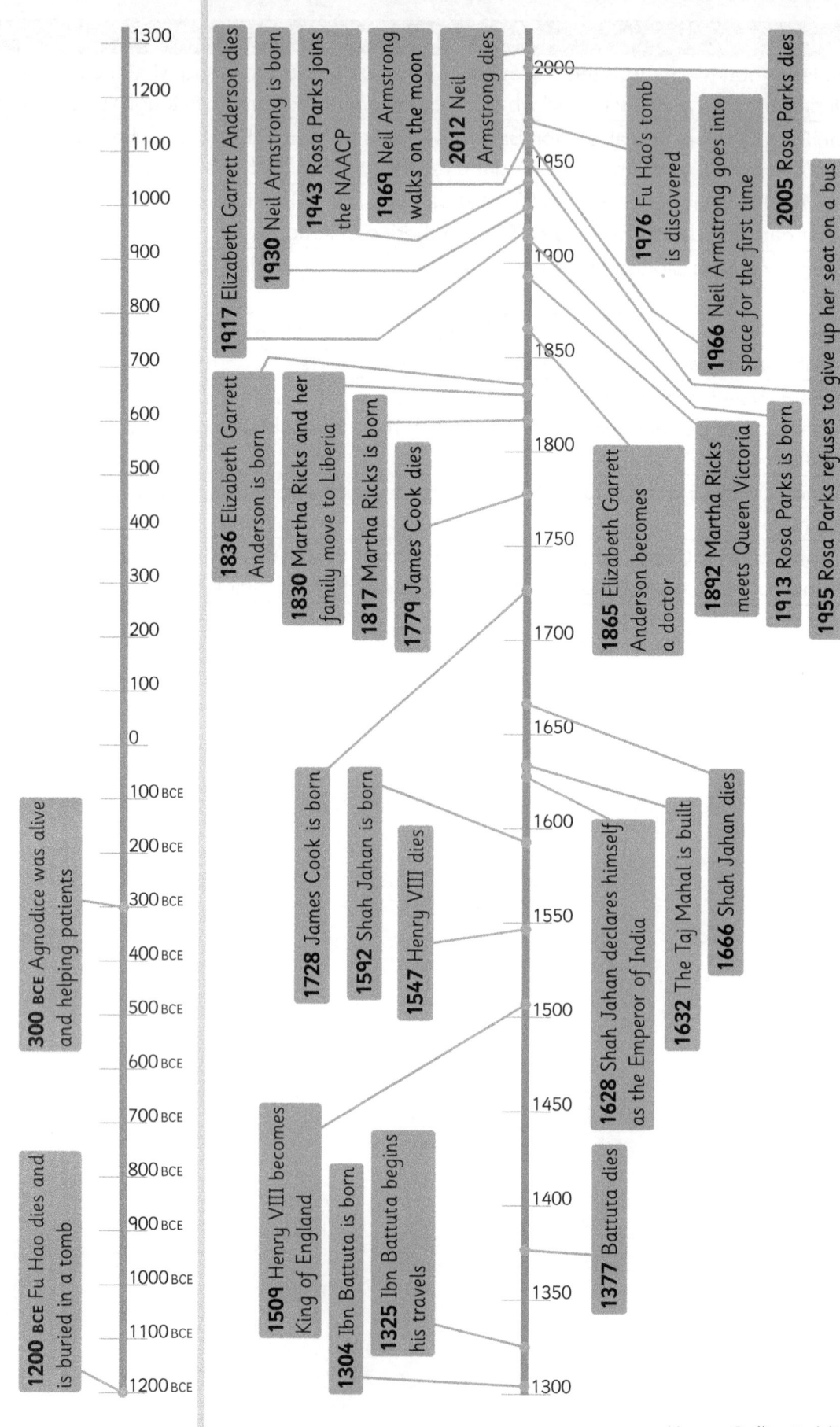

- **1200 BCE** Fu Hao dies and is buried in a tomb
- **300 BCE** Agnodice was alive and helping patients
- **1304** Ibn Battuta is born
- **1325** Ibn Battuta begins his travels
- **1377** Battuta dies
- **1509** Henry VIII becomes King of England
- **1547** Henry VIII dies
- **1592** Shah Jahan is born
- **1628** Shah Jahan declares himself as the Emperor of India
- **1632** The Taj Mahal is built
- **1666** Shah Jahan dies
- **1728** James Cook is born
- **1779** James Cook dies
- **1817** Martha Ricks is born
- **1830** Martha Ricks and her family move to Liberia
- **1836** Elizabeth Garrett Anderson is born
- **1865** Elizabeth Garrett Anderson becomes a doctor
- **1892** Martha Ricks meets Queen Victoria
- **1913** Rosa Parks is born
- **1917** Elizabeth Garrett Anderson dies
- **1930** Neil Armstrong is born
- **1943** Rosa Parks joins the NAACP
- **1955** Rosa Parks refuses to give up her seat on a bus
- **1966** Neil Armstrong goes into space for the first time
- **1969** Neil Armstrong walks on the moon
- **1976** Fu Hao's tomb is discovered
- **2005** Rosa Parks dies
- **2012** Neil Armstrong dies

HarperCollins*Publishers* 2019

Knowledge organiser and skills grid

Knowledge organiser

Some suggested steps for helping the pupils to produce a simple knowledge organiser:

- Focus on one person.
- What did this person do that was important or memorable?
- Where did they live?
- When did they live? (that is, when were they born and when did they die?)
- What was going on at that time?
- How did they change what was happening at the time?
- What evidence did we use to find out about them? (for example visual images, artefacts/objects, documents – letters, diaries, newspapers, maps and so on)
- How do we remember them? How should we remember them?

Skills grid

Activity	History skills targeted
Ordering photographs (for example Rosa Park's life)	Chronological Understanding
Placing the person on the class timeline	Chronological Understanding
Using appropriate vocabulary relating to the passage of time	Chronological Understanding
Examining and discussing evidence (sources of information) for example an image (for example Henry VIII image activity), document	Historical Enquiry
Asking and answering questions	Knowledge and Understanding
Be able to recognise what is evidence and sources of information	Knowledge and Understanding and Historical Enquiry
Giving simple opinions	Knowledge and Understanding and Historical Interpretation
Annotating an image	Historical Interpretation

Teaching about significant individuals to pupils aged 5–7

Young children enjoy finding out about people from all walks of life. As teachers, we can capitalise on this by helping them to appreciate some of the characteristics of significant people and how these people help others and benefit society.

Who is 'significant'?

With older pupils you could consider who is famous and who is significant, perhaps using local examples that the class is familiar with. Ian Dawson's definition can be used to help pupils make their own decisions about this.

Reasons for a person being significant – if she or he:

- changed events at the time they lived
- improved lots of people's lives – or made them worse
- changed people's ideas
- had a long lasting impact on their country or the world
- had been a really good, or a very bad example to other people of how to live or behave.

(Dawson 2003)

Encourage your pupils to use this framework with every new person they learn about; this will enable them to appreciate that they can use knowledge or processes learned in a previous topic and they are not starting from scratch every time.

Context and comparisons

In order to understand the lives of the people you teach about; younger pupils need to be able to place them in a historical context with some basic knowledge about the era they lived in. Some of the significant people you choose to teach about may be still alive but teaching about individuals enables us to help pupils understand and compare aspects of life in different periods. If you teach about two contrasting individuals together, then give a clear context for making suitable comparisons about their lives.

Suggested activities

The emphasis here needs to be on using primary sources that the class can access. This would usually be visual images, artefacts and simple documents. Two or three well-chosen images which illustrate the person and what they did, or the time period in which they lived, can be successfully used. Careful questioning can draw pupils' attention to the similarities and differences they can see to their own lives. Where available, they could order a series of pictures of the person's life, or a significant event in their life, into chronological order to begin to appreciate that we all start out as babies and grow up.

Original artefacts which the person actually used would be almost impossible to source, but similar items could be presented in a suitcase and then discussed with the class to show the kind of person they were. This could be used as an introductory activity to hook them into the topic.

Documents are often written by hand and consequently can be difficult for younger children to read. One way round this can be to provide a typed transcript but it is a good idea to provide a copy of the original to avoid misconceptions about printers and computers being available then. Even young children enjoy being 'detectives' and trying to find words they recognise in an old piece of writing. You also need to make a judgement about how complicated, and how much information is presented on the page.

In addition, activities such as role play and drama could be used to develop children's empathy. An adult could 'become' the person or someone close to the person, so the class has someone who they can ask questions of and explore what that person did (hot seating). Caution is needed in using drama with children of this age until they have a good grasp of the era the person lived in or misconceptions can be created and entrenched.

Using short video clips or podcasts/audio of the actual person speaking or moving can support pupils in beginning to understand that these were real people and are not just fictional characters in a book.
This is especially important with younger children as they may not appreciate that Snow White is a fictional character, but that Elizabeth Garrett Anderson is not!

Skills

All these activities will support pupils in developing the skills of historical enquiry and interpretation. They will learn to answer questions and also ask their own, begin to consider evidence and think critically. They will be beginning to understand cause and consequence, identifying similarities and differences and develop a personal 'big picture' of chronology.

Above all, try to make the experience fun and engaging so pupils are curious to find out more!

Resource sheet: Rosa Parks – Character evaluation line

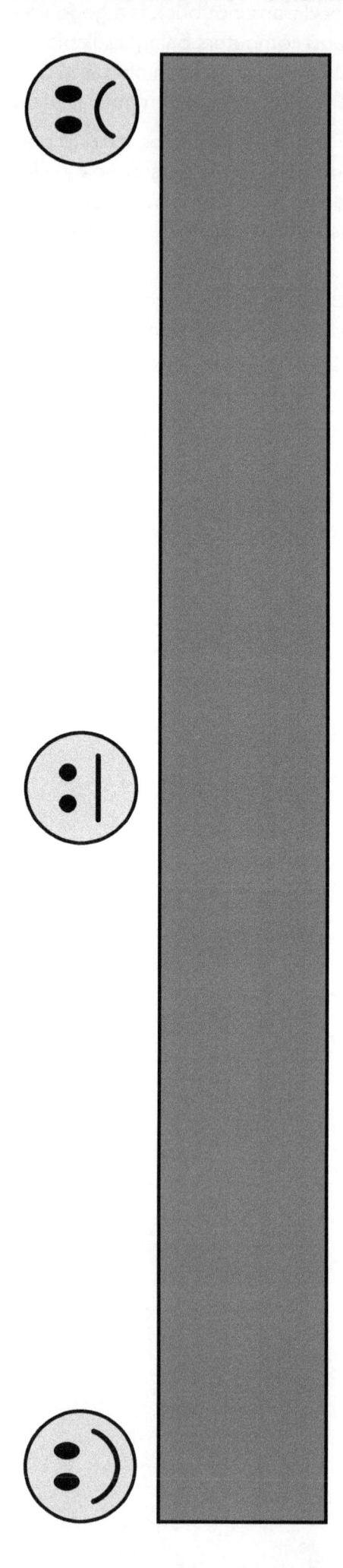

| Had a brother called Sylvester |

| Refused to give up her seat to a white man |

| Was an African-American woman |

| Set up a charity to help teenagers get career and vocational training |

| Lived in Montgomery, USA |

| Loved learning and studied hard at school |

| Left school aged 16 to care for her dying grandmother and very ill mother |

| Never paid the fine for refusing to give up her seat |

| Said what she thought |

✂---

Character line: Rosa Parks

Cut out the statements. Each small group of children (no more than four) has an A3 copy of the character line image and a set of the cards. Ask the children to consider each statement about the person and place it on the line showing whether the statement shows they are a good person, bad person or neutral. This activity could also be used to evaluate a king or queen or an event.

HarperCollins*Publishers* 2019

Resource sheet: Henry VIII – Examining a portrait

Henry VIII – Hans Holbein's painting 1537

Henry VIII

Paintings, especially portraits, are important historical sources. This activity supports pupils to examine a portrait 'like a historian', looking at the way the person is presented and why that might be. This will help pupils assess how useful the portrait is as a source.

Below are some questions you could ask your class, with possible answers, and further information, in parentheses.

Look at the person in the painting

- Who is he? (Henry VIII)
- What is his job? (King of England (not Scotland or Ireland))

Look at his face

- How old do you think he is? (He was 46 – do pupils think he looks 46? He was deliberately depicted as younger.)
- How do you think he might be feeling?
- What is he wearing on his head? (Hat decorated with fur and jewels and pearls to show off his wealth)
- Why isn't he smiling? (He needs to show he is serious, important)

Look at his body and clothes

- How is he standing? How does standing like this make you feel? (He is standing like a wrestler or warrior – it is a strong pose)
- Look at his shoulders – could they really be this big? (They have been exaggerated to make him seem more impressive)
- What is he wearing round his neck? (A chain with jewels – showing off his wealth and importance)
- What is holding in his hands? (Gloves and short dagger – shows he's ready for anything)
- How many rings is he wearing? (Wealth again)
- Henry had an accident shortly before this picture was painted – is there any evidence of this in the portrait? (No, because he wanted to look strong and healthy).

Look at the background

- Where might he be? (Inside a palace or rich home – tapestries on the walls. This is probably in his private quarters where few people were allowed to go)
- What is he carrying to represent stormy/bad weather? (Gloves – but they also signify he's ready for anything)
- Where is he looking? (Straight at the painter or the viewer – this was painted when his son Edward had just been born so sending a message to his people)

This portrait has been described as a piece of propaganda as so much has been exaggerated or emphasised. It deliberately shows him as an imposing, majestic figure in the best of health.

HarperCollins*Publishers* 2019

Resource sheet: Rosa Parks – Ordering photographs

Rosa Parks

Cut out the photographs and give to pupils to arrange in chronological order.

Ask pupils questions like:

Which picture was taken earliest in her life?

Why do you think we do not have any photographs of her as a baby or young child?

Why are there lots of photographs of her as an adult?

Pupil Book model answers

What to look for to ensure progression and understanding

Chronological understanding

In history there is rarely a 'right' or 'wrong' answer – as a teacher you are encouraging the class to develop their understanding of how we know about the past, and the job of a historian/archaeologist. In order to develop pupils' knowledge and understanding, you need to be asking lots of questions which help pupils to think about the sources of information you are using; the sources. Who wrote this? When was it written? How did they know this? Why was it recorded? Where was it written? Compare sources – What is the same? What is different? What has been left out? Why?

Adding information to the class timeline and encouraging them to use appropriate vocabulary (before, after, then, now, decade and so on) and ordering events in the life of an interviewee will help your pupils to begin to have an appreciation of what happened when – this will not be completely developed at this stage but we need to support and encourage this from the start of their education.

Knowledge and understanding

In order to ensure that your pupils' understanding is secure, encourage them to ask their own questions as well as answer your questions. Encouraging them to use When? Who? Why? Where? How? as question starters will help to scaffold this important skill. Young children also need to develop their chronological understanding gradually. This can start with photographs of a real person to put in order of their life (see the Rosa Parks – Ordering photography activity) or putting your significant individual on your class timeline. You can then build on this, helping pupils to start to understand timelines of various intervals and a variety of ordering activities to embed this skill.

Using sources

Even young children can begin to evaluate the sources they are using (such as the Henry VIII – Examining a portrait activity) and this can set the foundations for using these skills when, for example, searching for information on the internet in later life. It can be useful to evaluate sources in terms of the three Rs –

Rich – how much detail or information does it give you?

Relevant – is the information useful for this activity?

Reliable – where has the information come from, who produced the source? Why was the source created?

Historical interpretation

This skill can be challenging for teachers. It might help to think about what a real historian does – they examine sources and make educated guesses – justifying their guesses from what they know. At its simplest, this is what we want our pupils to be doing. So when they examine Henry VIII's portrait, they are looking for clues about what this tells us about him. Annotating an image is also asking for simple opinions so stretch more able pupils by asking for their justifications too – why do they think that? The Character line about Rosa Parks is a way of evaluating statements and can be adapted for any significant individual.

Above all, have fun with your pupils – your enthusiasm and encouragement are the key things in developing a love for history.

Teaching history to pupils aged 7–11

Stone Age to Iron Age

Topic introduction: Stone Age to Iron Age

Stone Age to Iron Age covers a very long time – over 10,000 years. The period is known as 'prehistory,' that is, before history, as there are no written sources. Nearly all the information we have about the period comes from the work of archaeologists and the artefacts that remain. Towards the end of the period, around Roman times, there are a few written sources to help us.

In some ways there are huge changes during this time – from many people changing from hunter-gatherer nomads to farmers; from using stone tools to using metal tools. The population of Britain grows, from around 5000 people at the start of the Mesolithic period (the Middle Stone Age) to perhaps 1 million people when Julius Caesar first comes to Britain in 55 BCE.

Many things stay the same, however. People mostly live in small groups or villages, not towns. Houses are mostly – but not always - made of wood and thatch. Life is uncertain and depends on the supply of food, which in turn often depends on the weather.

Perhaps the most exciting thing about studying this period is how our understanding of the time keeps changing, as new discoveries are made. Howick House in Northumberland, for example, was home to a group of hunter-gatherers in Mesolithic times. Hunter-gatherers follow animals and hunt, yet people seem to have lived in this house continuously. How do we explain that? More recently, excavations at Must Farm near Peterborough (which some are calling 'Britain's Pompeii'), have completely changed our view of life in the Bronze Age.

These changing ideas make it both exciting and complicated to study this period. Of course, for most questions there is no single right answer, so pupils are free to speculate and use the evidence to reach their own conclusion.

Overview of Pupil Book contents

Unit	Content
1	Prehistory. How the work of archaeologists helps us find out about events long ago. The chronology of the period. How ideas change .
2	Hunter-gatherers – how we know about their lives. Why our ideas change as new evidence is discovered. What was it like living in the Mesolithic Age?
3	The first farmers – Neolithic times. Why were women so strong? What kind of houses did the first farmers live in? What tools did they use? What was new about the New Stone Age?
4	Deaths and burials. How did Stone Age people commemorate the dead? Why was Stonehenge so important? How did it change over 1000 years? Is Stonehenge still significant today?
5	The Bronze Age – why was metal so important? How did it change things, and how do we know? What was it like living in the Bronze Age?
6	The Iron Age – when did iron come to Britain? How did iron change things? How useful is a modern reconstruction of an Iron Age village? How was Britain linked to the rest of the world at this time? The role of story and myth in Iron Age society.
7	Weapons and warfare – and how do we know? Were hill forts really forts? Why do historians disagree about hill forts? Why did the Romans come to Britain?
8	Prehistory – or history? – the story of Pytheas the Greek. Comparing Stone Age, Bronze Age and Iron Age. To what extent did life change over the period we have been studying in this book?
9	Looking at the wider picture: 1. Write your own Stone Age story 2. History and Art – what can we tell from cave paintings? 3. Bronze around the world 4. What did people use for money?

HarperCollins*Publishers* 2019

Knowledge organiser and skills grid

Knowledge organiser

Some key facts about Stone Age to Iron Age:

- It was a very long time ago. The period is known as 'Prehistory', because there are no written sources.
- It lasted a very long time – from the Ice Age around 11000 BCE to the coming of the Romans in 43 CE.
- In some ways there was little change. Houses, for example, stayed very much the same.
- In other ways things changed a great deal – from hunter-gathering to farming; from tools and weapons made of stone to tools and weapons made of bronze and then iron.
- Britain's population grew from perhaps 5000 people in the Mesolithic period to around 1 million by the end of the Iron Age.
- By the end of the Iron Age, Britain was a very wealthy country trading with the Romans and the rest of the world.
- Historians and archaeologists disagree about much of the evidence we have discovered about the period.
- New evidence is being discovered all the time, some of which changes what we think about the period.
- Re-enactors, like those at Butser Iron Age Farm, for example, can help us get a feel for what it was like living at the time.
- There are some places – Skara Brae, Stonehenge, Maiden Hill Fort, Grime's Graves for example – and some people – Cheddar Man, Amesbury Archer, Lindow Man for example – that are worth studying in some detail.

Skills grid

Unit	History skills targeted
Unit 1	Chronology, sense of period
Unit 2	Using historical knowledge to reach a conclusion
Unit 3	Continuity and change
Unit 4	Significance
Unit 5	Similarity and difference
Unit 6	Causation
Unit 7	Interpretations
Unit 8	Writing a focused account, presenting a conclusion

Additional resources: Stone Age to Iron Age

- Star Carr, *Life in Britain After the Ice Age*, Council for British Archaeology (for teachers)
- Barry Cunliffe, *Britain Begins*, Oxford University Press (for teachers)
- Kathleen Fidler, *The Boy with the Bronze Axe*, Kelpies Classics
- Clare Hibbert, *50 Things you should know about Prehistoric Britain*, QED Publishing
- Charlotte Hurdman, *Step into the Stone Age*, Southwater
- Robert Lacey, *Great Tales from English History*, volume 1, Little, Brown
- Sally Prue, *The Song Hunter*, Oxford University Press
- Francis Pryor, *Home – A Time Traveller's Tales From Britain's Prehistory*, Penguin Books (for teachers])
- Francis Pryor, Hilary Morris and Wessex Archaeology, 'Stone Age to Iron Age – overview and depth', *Primary History*, 66.
- Rethinking the Stone Age to Bronze Age, *Primary History*, 81.
- Film: Iron Age Farm, www.history.org.uk Search 'Iron Age Farm'.
- Prehistoric – BBC Bitesize, www.bbc.com/bitesize/topics/z82hsbk
- Timeline: Stone Age to Iron Age, historicengland.org.uk and search 'stone age to iron age timeline'.
- BBC History website, www.bbc.co.uk/history/british/timeline/neolithic_timeline
- The British Museum – search 'Prehistoric Britain', www.Britishmuseum.org
- Stone Age to Iron Age pottery replicas, www.tts-international.com
- BBC, 'Ancient Voices', www.bbc.co.uk, search 'Ancient Voices'.
- Scheme of Work – Stone Age to Bronze Age, www.history.org.uk/primary/resource/7537/scheme-of-work-stone-age-to-iron-age
- BBC, *The Story of Britain*, www.bbc.co.uk/programmes/p01z2nn3

Collins Big Cat books available at www.collins.co.uk:
- Collins Big Cat – *Life and Death in an Iron Age Hill Fort* (Copper)
- Collins Big Cat – *Skara Brae* (Turquoise)
- Collins Big Cat – *The Celts* (Ruby)
- Collins Big Cat – *The Stone Age* (Copper)
- Collins Big Cat – *Time-Traveller's Guide to the Bronze Age* (Sapphire)

Getting better at history: Stone Age to Iron Age

Deeper understanding of more complex issues and of abstract ideas

History is complicated and, as they get more confident, pupils should understand that people react in different ways in the same situation and begin to make use of that understanding in their work. There is usually no simple answer to historical problems, and understanding that is a sign of increasing historical maturity.

Let's think about continuity and change from the Mesolithic period to the Iron Age. Perhaps it is easier for pupils to think about change – from hunting to farming, from stone tools to bronze, then iron tools. But when archaeologists look at Iron Age burial sites, they often find both bronze and stone artefacts as well as iron ones. So how complete was the 'change' from one to the other? Did it happen slowly, spreading from one place to another, or did it happen quickly – lots of places adopting the new ways at more or less the same time? You can see how trying to answer this kind of question involves quite complicated thinking about change. This is what we mean by a 'deeper understanding….'

The same applies to continuity. Apart from Skara Brae, where there were no trees, virtually all houses throughout this period were made of timber and thatch. There were few, if any, windows, and the chimney was a hole in the roof. Doors usually faced east, to greet the morning sun. And yet Howick House is a very different shape to later houses, and Iron Age houses suddenly become round. There is continuity in the materials used in building houses, but change in shape and size. This is a good example of continuity and change appearing together.

Resource sheet: Unit 2.3 – Let's do it! questions 2–3

Look back over the work you have done throughout this unit. Make a list of everything you have discovered about life in the Mesolithic period. Sort your list carefully into the table below.

Where evidence agrees	Where evidence disagrees
	Mesolithic people moved around most of the time, yet Howick House seems to have been lived in permanently.

HarperCollins*Publishers* 2019

Resource sheet: Unit 3.2 – Let's do it! question 2

Look at the pictures of the house at Skara Brae and at Kingsmead Quarry. Make a list of similarities and differences between them in the table below. Do some further research about both houses if possible.

Ways the houses are similar	Ways the houses are different
	One is made of wood and the other is made of stone

HarperCollins*Publishers* 2019

Resource sheet: Unit 3.3 – Let's do it!

Look back carefully over the work you have done in Units 2 and 3 (the Mesolithic and the Neolithic periods), and fill in the table.

Continuity	Change
People still needed to work hard to feed everyone.	Kept animals rather than hunted them for food.

Which of the two columns is the most important? Think about whether there was more 'continuity' or more 'change'. That will help you structure your answer. There is no right answer — it depends on the evidence you use to support your ideas.

....

....

....

....

....

Resource sheet: Unit 7.2 – Let's do it! questions 4–5

Use the information in Units 6 and 7 to decide which of the interpretations shown in the first row of the table you think best fits what you know about hill forts.

'These large defensive enclosures protected by a series of steep ditches, can usually be found occupying prominent hilltop positions. In times of attack the local people may have sought refuge within the hillforts.'	'As monuments, they may have been as much about displaying the status and power of different community groups. as they were about defence.'	'Archaeologists have found evidence of housing and of ritual practices inside hill forts as well as storage of large amounts of grain.'
Ravensburgh Castle in Hertfordshire had a rampart nearly 14 metres high.		Weddings were arranged there.

I find interpretation (1)(2)(3) most likely to be accurate, because…

....

....

....

....

HarperCollins*Publishers* 2019

Pupil Book model answers

Unit 5.2, Think about it! question 1 asks: 'Why do you think some people called the archer ' King of Stonehenge'?'

This exercise is intended to give pupils an opportunity to use evidence to support a conclusion. When assessing their answers, here are some points to look for:

The introduction needs to set the scene – the grave, what was in it, when it was found – a simple description will do.

Then pupils can speculate about his origins – in the Alps – and his occupation – was he an archer, or a blacksmith, or both? They could go on to discuss his wealth – was he rich? Do the contents of his grave (copper knives and gold objects) **prove** he was rich?

Next, they should think about the idea of him being a king. What do kings do? Is there evidence that they had kings in the Bronze Age? (They obviously had leaders, but does that make him a king?) He was probably very important – anyone who knew how to make bronze and bronze tools at the time would be very special.

Finally, there should be a conclusion. There is no direct evidence that he was a king, but given the items and wealth in his grave he was obviously a very important person at the time – or were **all** Bronze Age people buried with items like this?

Unit 8.3 asks 'Of all these four periods – Mesolithic, Neolithic, Bronze and Iron – which one would you prefer to live in if you were given the choice? under the heading 'Finishing off your study of Stone Age to Iron Age'.

This exercise gives pupils an opportunity to write a focused account/present a conclusion.

There is no right or wrong answer to this question – each period has its advantages and its disadvantages. What we are looking for is a carefully planned answer using what the pupil **knows** to answer the question. It might be a balanced period by period advantages/disadvantages answer, or it might be a carefully argued statement about just one period. The key thing is the use of evidence to support their view. Two example answers are given below:

> 'I would rather live in the Iron Age. Hoards that have been excavated show some people were very rich. Hill Forts provided security from enemies. Iron tools like axes and sickles made clearing new fields and harvesting crops much easier. Trade with Europe brought in luxury goods. The rotary quern made grinding corn easier and life better for women and spinning and weaving made woollen clothes better and warmer.'

> 'It is difficult to decide when I would have preferred to live. Houses were pretty much the same in all periods – dirty, dark, small. Work was mostly farming in the Neolithic, Bronze and Iron Ages rather than hunting in the Mesolithic, although iron tools would probably make it easier. People would have been faced with the same problems of keeping warm, getting enough to eat and surviving **whenever** they lived.'

Invaders

Topic introduction: Invaders

Even before the Romans came to Britain, they knew how wealthy the country was. Trade with Europe was extensive, and Iron Age leaders had developed a taste for Roman luxuries. Britain was called the 'Tin Isles' by the Ancient Greeks and was the most important source of tin in the world. Britain was an attractive place to live!

The Romans wanted to add Britain to their empire, which was the largest the world had seen up to that time. They brought roads and villas, town life and a powerful army. They also, for about 400 years, brought peace. When the Roman army left to defend Rome from the barbarian invasion, Anglo-Saxons from Jutland and north west Europe decided Britain was a good place to live. Migrants settled mostly in the east and south of the country, living in villages and working as farmers. They also brought monks and nuns, as the Christian religion spread throughout Britain.

Finally, the Vikings came – first as raiders then as invaders, finally as settlers. Despite the efforts of Alfred the Great, England was divided between the Danelaw, where the Danes or Vikings ruled from York, and the rest of the country where the Saxons ruled from Winchester. Finally, after much fighting, England was united into one country and in the 11th century, there were Viking kings, like Cnut, who ruled the whole country.

This unit covers over 1000 years, from the arrival of the Romans to the defeat of the Anglo-Saxons by William the Conqueror in 1066 CE. How had England changed in that time? Was it still rich? Was it still a desirable place to live? Why did each of these peoples leave home and decide to come and settle in England? And what impact did they have on the English people and their way of life?

Overview of Pupil Book contents

Unit	Content
1	Coming to Britain – now and in the past. Why did the Romans, Anglo-Saxons and Vikings come to Britain? 'Push' and 'pull' factors of migration.
2	The unbeatable Roman army. Why did Boudicca rebel against the Romans? Making Britannia secure – building Hadrian's Wall. Did the Romans conquer Scotland?
3	Roman Britain; living in the town and in the countryside. Trade with the rest of the Roman Empire. Christians and Pagans. Why did the Romans leave?
4	What happened to Roman Britain after the Romans left? Who were the Anglo-Saxons? How did they make a living? What did Anglo-Saxon women do? Reconstructing history – King Arthur and West Stow Anglo-Saxon Village.
5	Anglo-Saxon town life. Why bury goods and not come back for them? Monks and Nuns. Was Alfred the Great the first King of all England?
6	The Vikings at home in Scandinavia. Raiders then settlers. The 'Great Heathen Army' arrives in England. Viking York – how do we know what it was like?
7	The Viking world – ships and trade. Fighting for England. The Danelaw. King Alfred defeats the Vikings. Cnut becomes King of England. How do we know about the Vikings, especially as they left virtually no written evidence?
8	Change between 43 CE and 1066 CE – what changed, and what stayed the same? When would you have rather lived – in Roman, Anglo-Saxon or Viking times? Why?
9	Looking at the wider picture: 1. History and Technology – warfare through the ages 2. History and English – drawing inferences 3. Empires and colonies

HarperCollins*Publishers* 2019

Knowledge organiser and skills grid

Knowledge organiser

Some key facts about Invaders:

- There are lots of reasons for people to move from one country to another.
- The Romans had the most powerful army, and the biggest empire, the world had seen at that time.
- Not all Britons welcomed the Romans. Boudicca, for example, led a massive revolt against the Romans.
- Roman Britain was very peaceful and very wealthy, with strong trading links with the rest of the world.
- When the Romans left, Anglo-Saxons came to live in Britain.
- Initially, historians called this the 'Dark Ages', suggesting that life was much worse than in Roman times.
- Religion was very important to the Anglo-Saxons. Monasteries grew up around the country.
- Most Anglo-Saxons lived in villages and farmed the land.
- England was so rich that the Vikings started to raid the country around 790 CE.
- Many decided to settle in Britain. This let to lots of fighting between Anglo-Saxons and Vikings over who runs the country.
- By 1014 CE there was a Viking King of England – King Cnut.
- Most historians refer to this period as the time when England became one united strong country.
- There were many changes between the Romans coming in 43 CE and the Norman invasion of 1066 CE.

Skills grid

Unit	History skills targeted
1	Chronology, causation
2	Diversity, evidence skills
3	Using evidence to reach a conclusion
4	Similarity and difference
5	Significance
6	Interpretations
7	Organising an enquiry and presenting a conclusion
8	Chronology, continuity and change

Additional resources: Invaders

- Christopher Culpin, *Viking Expansion*, Hodder Education (A GCSE textbook ideal for teachers)
- John Haywood, *Northmen*, Head of Zeus (for teachers)
- Robert Lacey *Great Tales from English History*, Volume 1, Little Brown
- 'The Roman Empire and its impact on Britain', *Primary History*, 70
- 'Britain's settlement by Anglo-Saxons and Scots', *Primary History*, 68
- 'Viking and Anglo-Saxon Struggle for the Kingdom of England', *Primary History*, 69
- Neil Oliver, *Vikings: A History*, Orion books (for teachers)
- Thorleif Sjovold, *The Viking Ships in Oslo*, Univeritetets Oldsaksamling
- West Stow Anglo-Saxon Village
- Bede's World, Jarrow
- Jorvik, Viking York
- Roman archaeo-box, TTS Group
- Anglo-Saxon archaeo-box, TTS Group
- Michael Wood's Story of England, Episode 1 – Romans to Normans (for teachers), www.bbc.co.uk/programmes and search 'Michael Wood Story of England'.
- An Introduction to Roman Britain, www.english-heritage.org.uk Search 'Story of England' and select the 'Romans' tab
- How the Romans conquered Britain, www.bbc.com and search for the title.
- An overview of Roman Britain (for teachers), www.bbc.co.uk/history/ancient/romans/questions_01.shtml
- How was Anglo-Saxon Britain ruled?, www.bbc.com and search for the title.
- 10 things you (probably) didn't know about the Anglo-Saxons, www.historyextra.com and search 'anglo saxons'
- Anglo Saxon royal rings, www.teachinghistory100.org and filter for 'KS2: Britain: Anglo-Saxons and Scots' and theme 'Rule and rulers'.
- Wychurst – Anglo Saxon re-enactment site, regia.org and click 'Wychurst'.
- Overview - the Vikings 800–1066, www.bbc.co.uk/history/ancient/vikings/overview_vikings_01.shtml
- What was life like in Viking Britain?, www.bbc.com and search for the title.
- The Vikings in Britain, a brief history, www.history.org.uk and search 'Vikings in Britain'.

Collins Big Cat books available at www.collins.co.uk:
- Collins Big Cat – *Boudica* (Emerald)
- Collins Big Cat – *Early Kings of England* (Ruby)
- Collins Big Cat – *How to be an Anglo Saxon* (Topaz)
- Collins Big Cat – *How to be a Roman* (Ruby)
- Collins Big Cat – *How to Be a Viking* (Copper)
- Collins Big Cat – *Julius Caesar* (Topaz)
- Collins Big Cat – *Roman Life in Britain* (Copper)
- Collins Big Cat – *Vikings in Britain* (Ruby)

Getting better at history: Invaders

Greater independence in applying the skills and concepts of history

Pupils should be becoming more able to ask their own questions of history, to decide how to find evidence, and how to present their conclusions; in other words, they should become more self-reliant in deciding how they investigate topics.

Invaders is an ideal topic to encourage self-reliance and independent study skills. You could, for example, use Unit 2.1 to teach about the Roman army and then later in the unit leave pupils to discover how similar and how different Anglo-Saxon and Viking armies were. Or you could use the images in unit 3.2 and 7.1 as the basis for an investigation into Roman, Anglo-Saxon and Viking ships and sailing techniques. In each of these examples, you are providing an initial stimulus and some scaffolding for less able pupils then encouraging children to devise their own questions and plan their own enquiry.

Older pupils can be left to decide the best way to present their conclusions once their enquiry is done – do they write an account, produce a poster, make a presentation or a web page? They should be able to decide for themselves which is most effective. Here are some suggested outcomes:

Oral Outcomes	Written Outcomes	Visual Outcomes
Presentation	Report	PowerPoint – picture selection
Debate	Letter/email	Documentary film – movie-maker
'Panel' discussion	Review	Web pages
Interview	Short biography	Exhibition gallery
Tour guide/audio presentation	Fictional story	Museum/gallery/site guide
Radio documentary	Web debate	Souvenir
Podcast	Text book spread	Model
Movie-maker commentary	Poem/song	Film/stage set
Hot seating	Blog	Board game
Speech to audience	Website text	Interactive display
Exhibition commentary	Trailer for a movie	Multi-media storyboard

Resource sheet: Unit 2.3 – Let's do it! question 1

Research the Antonine Wall and Hadrian's Wall and fill in the table.

	Antonine Wall	Hadrian's Wall
When was it built?		
Why was it built?		
What materials were used?		
How tall/How long was it?		
Anything else...?		

How similar were the two walls?

....

....

How different were the two walls?

....

....

Which do you think was more effective? Why?

....

....

HarperCollinsPublishers 2019

Resource sheet: Unit 6.3 – Let's do it! questions 1–2

Historians write about the Vikings in different ways. Why do we have such different interpretations of the Vikings?

Read these two extracts from a history book and a history article:

SOURCE 1 Extract from 'A History of the World for Young Readers', published in 1965

Rampaging Vikings, or Norsemen, from northern lands now known to us as Norway, Sweden, and Denmark, in their determination to entrench themselves as traders, merchants, and seamen at the earliest opportunity, overran the inviting territories of southern Europe, like a plague upon the inhabitants. Most Norsemen, it seems, were concerned with raiding and trading to the exclusion of all else. Not only did they raid the villages of the Holy Roman Empire, but they plundered and sacked seaports and remote hamlets along the shores of the Baltic and North seas. So fierce were these Norsemen that many of the priests were said to close their sermons with a prayer: "God, deliver us from the fury of the Northmen."

SOURCE 2 Extract from 'Vikings History: An Overview of the Culture and History of the Viking Age,' History on the Net

Vikings raided, traded and settled all along Europe's coasts. For 300 years, churches would pray to be spared the "wrath of the Norsemen." If the Vikings found an unprotected church or monastery, they'd raid. If they came to a well-defended town, they would trade. Early in the Viking Age, trade was done by direct barter. Eventually, Viking traders obtained a great deal of trade silver and Arabic coins, which then was used to buy goods.

Vikings established bases and trade centres in both Dublin and York. Many Viking craftsmen settled there. Their workshops produced cups, tableware, glass beads, pottery, glasses, bone and antler combs, leather goods, jewellery, and cloth. Blacksmiths and armour makers produced swords, battle axes, chainmail and armour.

During the Viking Age, Norsemen traded all up and down the coasts of 'Europe, establishing new homes in many locations... They settled on the Orkney, Shetland, Hebrides, Scilly Islands and Isle of Man. Eventually, these Vikings intermarried and settled in permanently...

How are these interpretations **similar** to each other?

How are they **different?**

What evidence does each author use to support their interpretation?

Do you know about any evidence that supports each interpretation?

Can you work out **why** the authors say such different things? (Clue — did the Vikings behave the same way from 793 to 1066?)

Which one do you find most accurate in describing the Vikings? Why?

Resource sheet: Unit 7.2 – Let's do it! question 1

Make a timeline of events you have read about from the raid on Lindisfarne to the death of King Cnut.

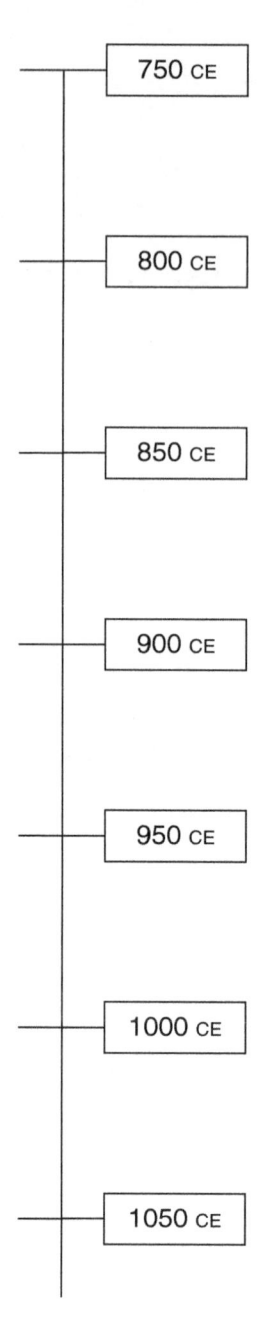

- 750 CE
- 800 CE
- 850 CE
- 900 CE
- 950 CE
- 1000 CE
- 1050 CE

Which do you think are the three most important events in all that time? Why?

....
....
....

Resource sheet: Unit 8.1 – Let's do it! questions 1–4

Complete the table below. Add your own categories to the column on the left. Decide whether you think these things were similar in Roman, Anglo-Saxon and Viking times, or different. Place a 'tick' in the appropriate box.

Category	Similar	Different

In your opinion, did things change most in Roman, Anglo-Saxon, or Viking times?

....

....

Pupil Book model answers

Unit 3.3, Think about it! question 2 asks *'Why might historians have thought the period after the Romans left was a 'Dark Age' for Britain?'.*

When assessing pupils' answers, here are some points to look for:

Historians used to call the period after the Romans left Britain the 'Dark Ages,' arguing that civilisation came to an end as the last Roman troop left around 410 CE.

There are three stages to answering this question. A good first step is to describe what the Romans brought to Britain. This includes roads, towns and cities, increased trade with the rest of Europe, and peace and stability. Most people were better off.

Next, pupils should think about what the Romans took away with them. Perhaps most important was the army that had protected Britain from invasion. Second was the links to Europe, again a benefit of being part of the Roman Empire.

Pupils should finish with a conclusion, deciding if that makes a 'Dark Age'. Did things change for most people? Pupils may conclude that many people carried on making a living in the same way, growing the same kind of food, making the same kinds of pots and pans, weapons and tools, trading with Europe, importing and exporting the kind of things they had for 400 years.

It is easy to see why some historians think that the Romans took away civilisation when they left – after all, it used to be said that the Celts, before the Romans came, were ignorant savages who painted themselves blue and fought each other all the time! And it was the Romans who made Britain wealthy.

Unit 4.1 uses the examples of Wroxeter, a Roman city; and Birdoswald Fort on Hadrian's Wall, that carried on much as before for over 200 years after the Romans left. Increasingly, historians are no longer talking of the Dark Ages when they describe Britain after the Romans left, suggesting that for many life went on pretty much as before. This question asks pupils to speculate about life after 410 CE – they will find out more about the so-called Dark Ages in Units 4 and 5.

Unit 5.3, Let's do it! question 2 gives pupils the following task: *'Research Alfred, or one of the other famous people discussed in Units 4 and 5. Make a presentation to your group on why they were significant'.*

To support pupils in creating their presentation, you could first discuss the steps below.

The first step in answering this question is to decide **how** to measure 'significance'. Pupils might find it easier if you use the term 'very special' or 'very useful'.

Ian Dawson, a well-known historian and history teacher, uses these criteria for deciding significance.

If it/a person:
- changed events at the time
- improved lots of people's lives – or made them worse
- changed people's ideas
- had a long-lasting impact on the country or the world
- had been a really good or a very bad example to other people of how to live or behave.

Is his criteria helpful in this instance? Perhaps *'improved lots of people's lives'* might be a useful starting point. For example, in what ways did King Alfred of Wessex improve life for the people of England? Do any of the other criteria apply?

You might broaden the discussion to include other ways the person was important – for example, for pupils researching Alfred: perhaps as an inspiration to others, in encouraging learning, in simplifying the laws, as well as protecting his lands from the Vikings?

The next step, once the criteria have been agreed, is to find out all the ways the person had an impact on the country or the world. For example, King Alfred had an impact on England – the 'burning the cakes' story; fighting the Vikings; securing the kingdom of Wessex; setting up fortified towns or 'burghs'; building a navy to fight the Vikings at sea as well as on land; and so on.

After that, it is important to make a judgement as to how much all these actions improved things both at the time, and later. For example, does Alfred deserve to be known as the King of all-England, as some people think? And is Alfred thought to be as significant today as in the 9th century?

Finally, pupils need to decide whether they think the person was a significant individual who had a huge impact on people in Anglo-Saxon and Viking times. Pupils who choose to research Alfred should consider the question 'why *do* we call Alfred 'the Great'? Only they can they decide whether *they* think he was a significant individual.

Unit 8.3, Think about it! question 1 asks *'If you had a time machine, which period would you choose to visit? Would you have preferred to live in Roman Britain, Anglo-Saxon Britain, or Viking Britain? Why?'*. Let's do it! questions 1–3 follow on from this activity.

This is very much a 'pull it all together' activity for which there is **no** correct answer. The best answers will use evidence effectively to support whichever conclusion they come to. The **range** of evidence used to support a conclusion will be important too – the best answers will have considered several aspects of life at the time, not just 'was it safe?' or 'was there enough to eat?' A grid like this might help pupils pull their ideas together before they start writing their answers:

	Good things	Bad things
Roman times		
Anglo-Saxon times		
Viking times		

HarperCollins*Publishers* 2019

Victorian Times

Topic introduction: Victorian Times

Victoria became Queen of Great Britain and Ireland in 1837 and died in 1901, so technically the Victorian period dates from that time. When she became Queen, most people in Britain lived in the countryside and worked in agriculture. When she died, most people lived in towns and cities and worked in industry. By 1901 Britain also had a huge empire covering every part of the globe. Britain was a superpower – it was a very, very rich country.

Not everyone in the country was rich, however. Many people were low paid and lived in awful slum houses. For much of the time, the Government didn't seem to care. They thought it was not the business of government to build houses or schools or look after people's health – that ought to be left to individuals to do for themselves. And most people – men or women – could not vote for the government so it was very difficult for ordinary people to get things changed.

Many historians call this period 'The Great Changes'. There were changes in transport – the railways for example; in work – steam powered machines in factories; in who could vote for the government – by 1901 around 66 per cent of men (but no women) could vote in elections. Going to school was compulsory after 1870, and free after 1891. Paid holidays began to appear for a few, and workers were often given Saturday afternoon off work. This led to the growth of football as a spectator sport. New inventions such as refrigeration, tinned food, electricity, typewriters and telephones began to change both work and life. Things definitely were not the same for everyone when Queen Victoria died as when she became Queen in 1837!

Overview of Pupil Book contents

Unit	Content
1	Who were the Victorians? Queen Victoria and Prince Albert. The 1851 Great Exhibition – what does it tell us about the Victorians?
2	Changes in the countryside. Living and working in the countryside. Changes in working methods during Queen Victoria's reign. What happened to poor people? Emigration.
3	Changes in the towns. Living and working in towns – how healthy were they? Were all towns the same? What was it like working in the new factories? How did some people try to make life better?
4	Changes in travelling. By rail and by sea – which new method of travelling had the greatest impact? Why were there so many horses in Victorian times?
5	Trade and empire. Why was having an empire so important? Why did people go abroad? How important was India to Britain? Was the British Empire a good thing?
6	Changes in leisure and recreation. What did the Victorians do for fun? How similar was it to what children do today?
7	Changes in rights. Who could vote in Victorian times? Why did people want the vote? What role did women play in Victorian life? Was it better to be a rich or a poor woman? What did workers do to try to improve their living and working conditions?
8	How inventive were the Victorians? How did communications change during Victorian times? Were people healthier in 1900 than in 1800? Does the Victorian period deserve to be known as 'The Great Changes'?
9	Looking at the wider picture: 1. History and maths 2. History and design and technology 3. Going to school around the world

Knowledge organiser and skills grid

Knowledge organiser

Some key facts about the Victorian Times:

- Victoria was Queen for over 60 years, from 1837 to 1901. During that time Britain became a very powerful country with a huge empire.
- Historians often call Victorian times the 'Great Changes'.
- By 1851 more people lived in towns and cities than in the countryside, and more worked in industry than in farming.
- Inventions changed life for many – steam power ran the new factories, and railways made travel much cheaper and faster.
- To begin with, life in the new towns and cities was very overcrowded, dirty and unhealthy. It took a long time for the Government to take action to make things better.
- More and more men were given the vote while Victoria was Queen, Britain was becoming more democratic – but women could not vote.
- People without jobs were encouraged to emigrate to the USA, Canada, Australia and New Zealand.
- More and more manufactured goods like cotton cloth and machines were exported; and more and more raw materials like raw cotton and food were imported.
- This time saw the growth of seaside resorts, professional sport and Music Halls and theatres.
- Throughout Victoria's reign many women fought hard for better rights – to keep their own money, to own their own house, to get a good education and to be able to vote.
- Going to school was made compulsory in 1870.
- Many people – but not everybody – were better off in 1901 than they had been in 1837.

Skills grid

Unit	History skills targeted
Unit 1	Sense of period, significant individual and event
Unit 2	Continuity and change
Unit 3	Cause and consequence
Unit 4	Similarity and difference
Unit 5	Continuity and change, interpretations
Unit 6	Using evidence to reach a conclusion
Unit 7	Making a comparison between units (Ancient Greece and Britain)
Unit 8	Presenting a clear and convincing argument

HarperCollins*Publishers* 2019

Additional resources: Victorian Times

- Kate Jackson Bedford, *Children in History: Victorians*, Franklin Watts
- Robert Lacey, *Great Tales from English History*, Volume 3, Little Brown
- Beamish Open-Air Museum, County Durham
- Black Country Museum, Dudley, West Midlands
- Feature film, *Oliver!* 1968, suitable for children
- Pathe News: 'Funeral of Queen Victoria', www.britishpathe.com and search 'Queen Victoria funeral'.
- Victorian Britain – a brief history, www.history.org.uk and search 'Victorian Britain'.
- What can you do with a Victorian trade directory?, www.history.org.uk and search 'Victorian trade directory'
- Victorians – the life of Mary Seacole, www.bbc.com and search 'Mary Seacole'.
- A series of radio programmes for children aged approximately 7 to 11, www.bbc.co.uk and search 'Primary History The Victorians'
- BBC History – the Victorians, www.bbc.co.uk/history/british/victorians/ (for teachers who want to improve their subject knowledge)
- The British Library – Victorian Britain, www.bl.uk/victorian-britain (for teachers who want to improve their subject knowledge)
- History Extra: The Victorians, www.historyextra.com and select 'Victorian' from the drop-down 'period' menu.
- A Victorian Christmas, www.historic-uk.com and search for title.
- History Cookbook – the Victorians, cookit.e2bn.org and select 'Victorians' from the 'History Cookbook' tab.
- 10 of the worst jobs in Victorian Britain, mentalfloss.com and search 'Victorian jobs'
- Songs of the Victorians, www.songsofthevictorians.com
- Walk through a Victorian House, www.geffrye-museum.org.uk and search 'Victorian house'.
- Blists Hill Victorian Town, www.ironbridge.org.uk and search 'Blists Hill'.

Collins Big Cat books available at www.collins.co.uk:
- Collins Big Cat – *Hard Times: Growing Up in the Victorian Age* (Diamond)
- Collins Big Cat – *How to be a Victorian in 16 Easy Stages* (Diamond)

Getting better at history: Victorian Times

Sharper methods of enquiry and communication

Evidence is the bedrock of history – without it, it is just 'story'. As they get older, pupils ought to be able to be more critical of evidence they find, asking questions such as, '*Why* does this person say that? Do I *trust* them? Another person says something different – how do I decide which one to believe?' Answers might be much less black and white, with nuances that reflect the differences in the evidence, or in historians' views.

In this book we introduce pupils to lots of evidence – both sources (dating from the time) and interpretations (produced much later). How do we help pupils to really 'squeeze' the evidence? Let's look at this source from unit 5.3. What does it tell us?

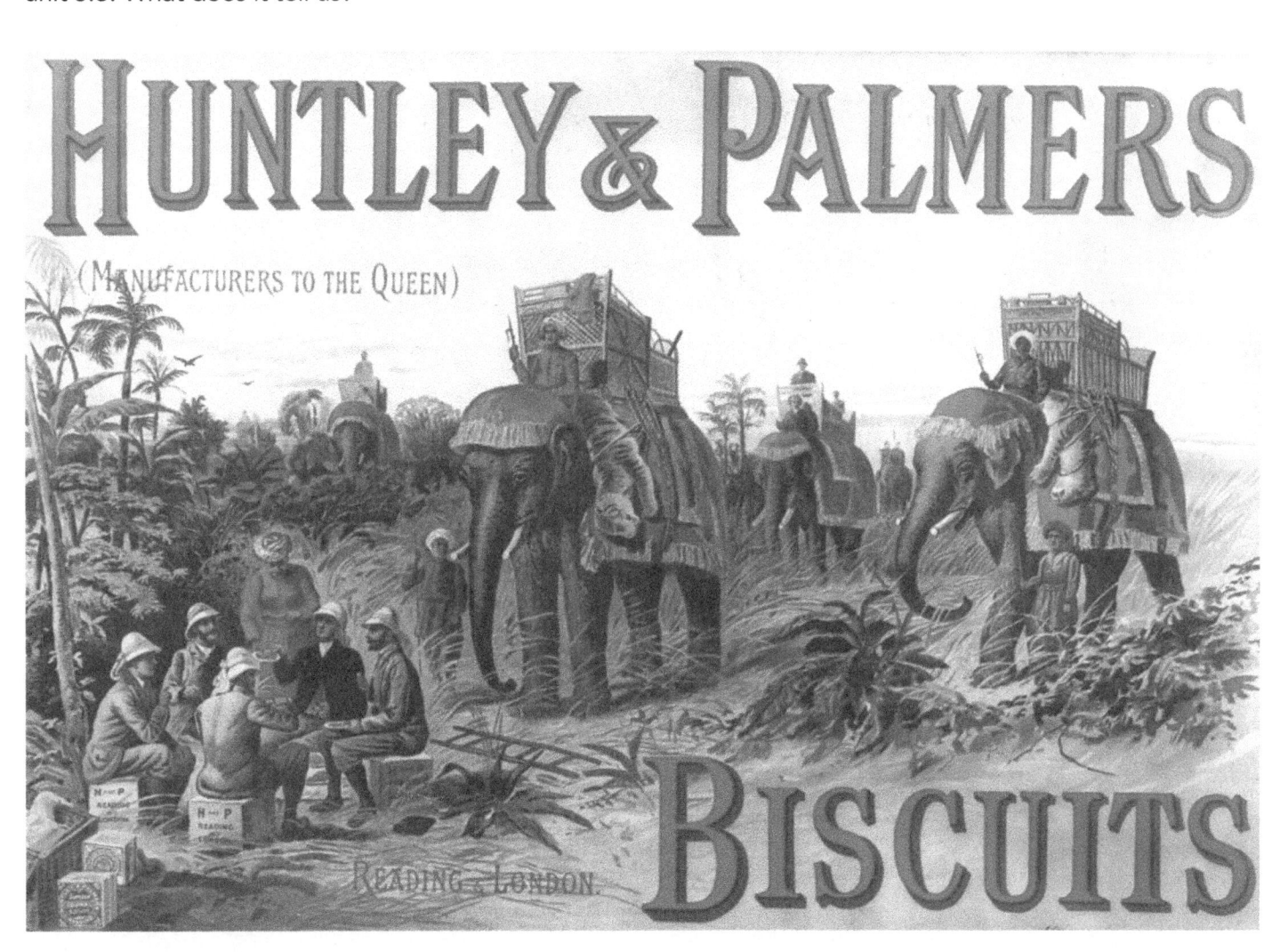

Useful questions to ask about it might include:

- What is it?
- What might it have been used for? How can you tell?
- How old is it?
- Why was it printed?
- Who is it aimed at?
- Where was it printed?

Once they have 'squeezed' all the information they can from the advert, pupils might begin to think about how *typical* it is. Questions might include:

- Are there other, similar, adverts that I know of?
- What does the advert tell us about Huntley and Palmer, the firm that makes the biscuits?
- What does the advert tell us about the British when they travel the world?
- What does the advert tell us about the British Empire?

Finally, pupils ought to be encouraged to reach a conclusion about this piece of evidence – how *useful* is it to the enquiry I am doing. What does it add to what I already know? Do I trust it? Also, they need to remember that sometimes we cannot find all the answers to our questions from one source.

The more we can move pupils away from 'reading evidence for information' towards being critical readers, the more successful they will be in studying history.

Resource sheet: Unit 3.1 – Let's do it! question 1

Look at this picture of a Glasgow courtyard in the 1860s. Label all the health hazards you can see. One has been done for you to get you started.

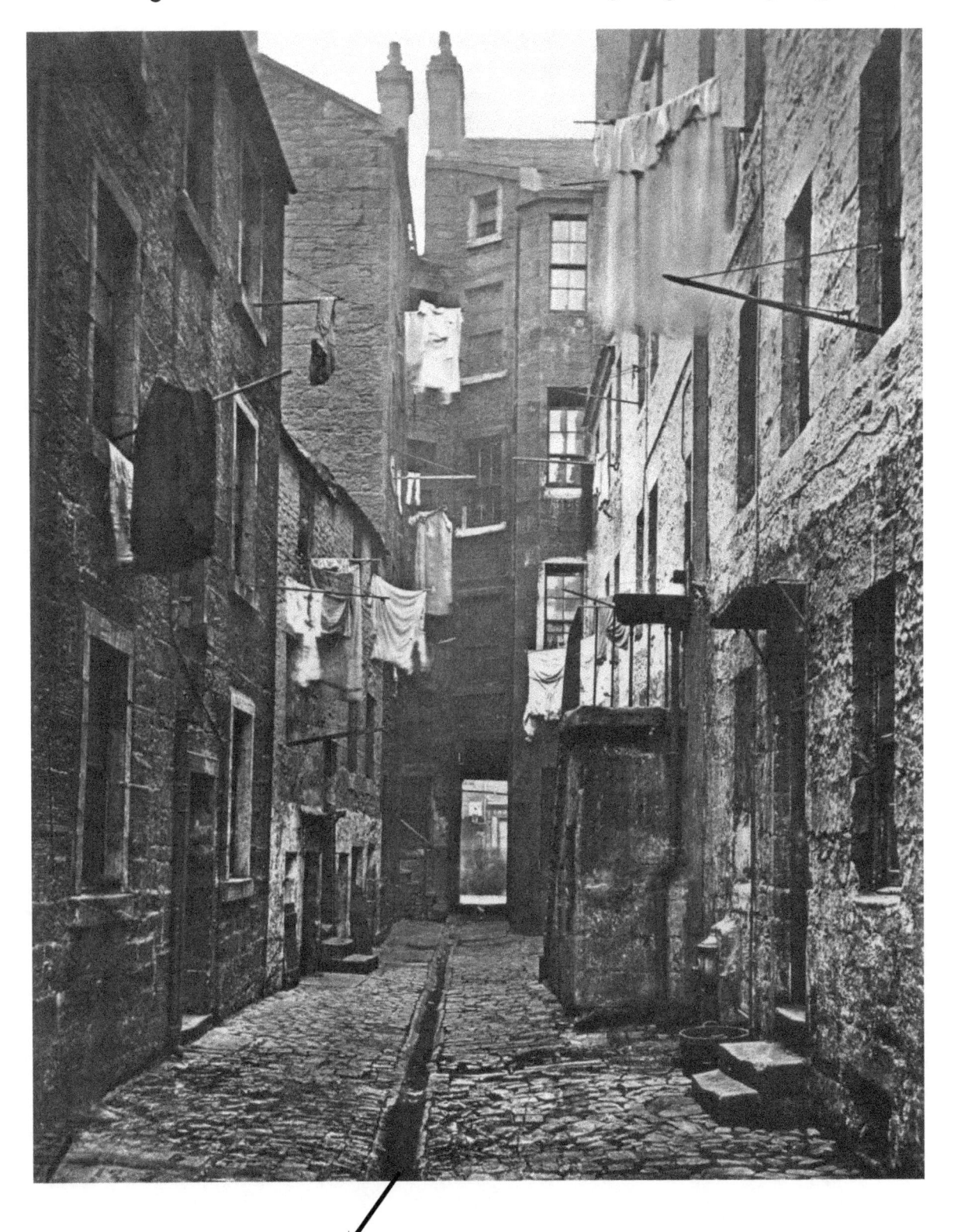

Open drain running down the middle of the walkway

Resource sheet: Unit 4.1 – Think about it! question 2

Look carefully at the picture of the Victorian seaside. Circle all the things that you *would not* see at the seaside today.

How similar is the Victorian seaside to the seaside today?

....

....

....

....

Resource sheet: Unit 5.3 – Let's do it! question 1

Load the scales, with all good things about the Empire on the '+' side, and all bad things on the '−' side. Which way do you think the scales will fall?

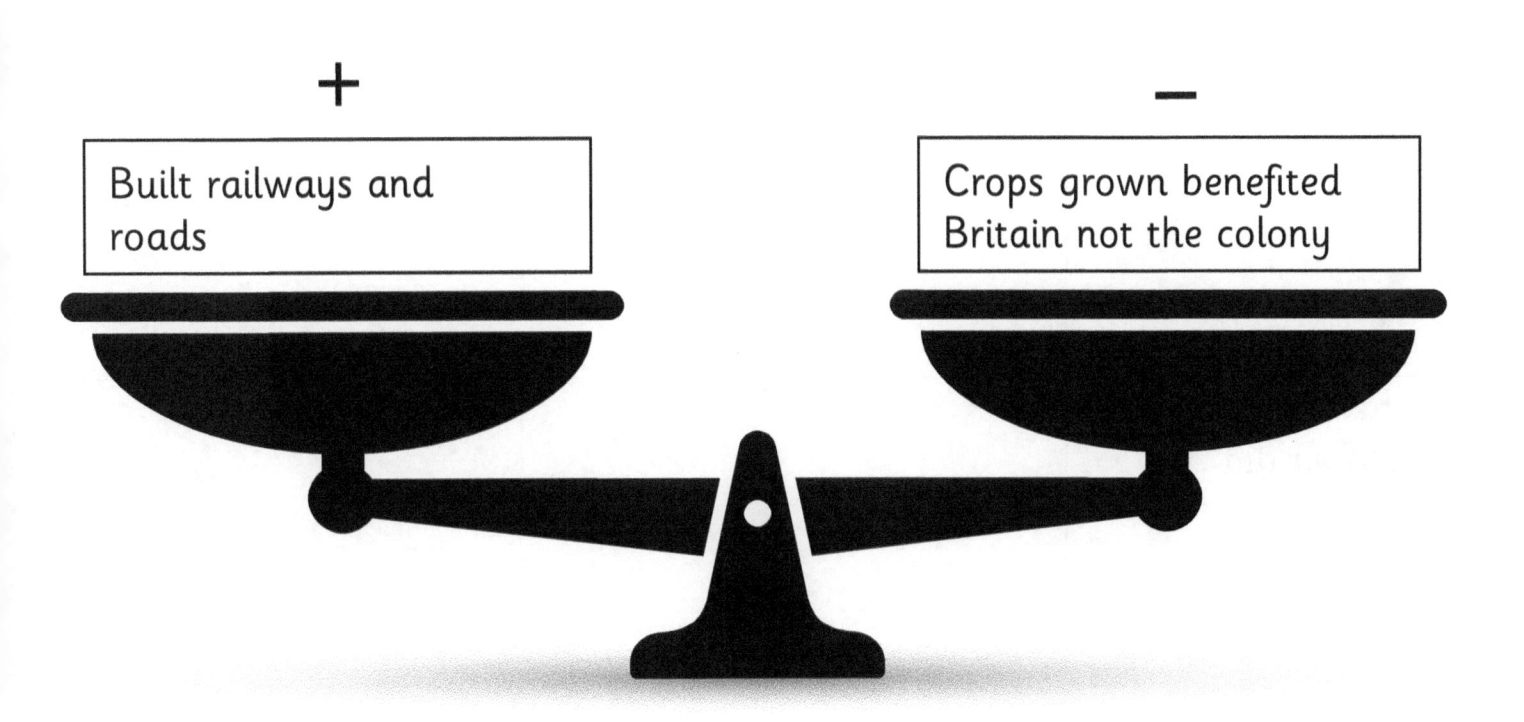

+

Built railways and roads

−

Crops grown benefited Britain not the colony

Resource sheet: Unit 6.2 – Think about it! question 1

How similar were Victorian entertainments to those we have today? Complete the table below.

	Similar to today	Different to today
entertainment		
games		
going to the fair		
going out		
staying in		
other things children did		

Pupil Book model answers

Unit 1.2, Let's do it! question 2 asks pupils to write a diary entry of a visit they might have made to the Exhibition.

This activity will encourage pupils to develop a sense of period. To support pupils in preparing to write their diary entries, you could first discuss the points below:

The key to this activity is selection – there were over 100,000 exhibits inside the Crystal Palace. Which would you choose to go to see? Which would interest you the most?

The other thing to be careful about is a sense of period – we don't want diary entries referring to someone outside the Great Exhibition selling modern fast food, or emailing a friend to tell them what they have seen!

You might collect together a series of images of the Great Exhibition – there are lots available – to prompt this activity.

Start with the journey to the Exhibition – by train perhaps, or walking. Ask: How long would it take? How much would it cost? What if you had never been on a train before? Which day would you go on? How much would it cost to get in? What would you think seeing the *outside* of the Exhibition? And what about the crowds – the sights, sounds, and smells – even the queue to get in.

Once inside the Great Exhibition, which exhibits would they choose to see – probably starting, like most people did, in the central area. What would be unusual – the elephant? The huge diamond? If you were a farmer, you might look at the new machinery. If you were a factory worker, you might want to see the fine linens and silks. And don't forget the public toilets – they were a real novelty.

Finally, as it is a diary entry, there ought to be some reflection on the day and of what had been seen. Remember this is 1851, when things were very different to today, and the Great Exhibition had lots of new and exciting things on show.

Unit 2.2, Let's do it! question 1 asks pupils to *'describe how working on a farm changed during Victorian time?'*. Question 2 asks *'Have some things on the farm stayed the same?'*.

This exercise looks at continuity and change.

Unit 2.1 paints a bleak picture of life in the countryside in the early 19th century, and Unit 2.2 highlights many of the changes that took place while Victoria was Queen. The 'Change' part of the answer is relatively easy – new crops, machines, bigger markets. The 'Continuity' is less easy, although some jobs, like milking the cows, were still done by hand.

To begin, they need to describe farming as it was – hard work, long hours, poor housing, and low pay. Ploughing was done by horses, harvesting with a scythe or sickle, women and children were working too. The fact that horses were treated better than workers says it all!

Next, they need to show the changes. Population grew so there was a demand for more food. Farmers could make a lot of money, so they invested in new technology. Reaping machines, steam ploughs and threshing machines were all quicker and cheaper. New crops were grown, and more animals kept.

Remember that at the end of the century things got tougher – competition from cheap food from abroad brought down prices and profits fell.

In conclusion, they need to think about 'how much' change there has been, and if it was for better or worse for farmers. Pupils should be encouraged to reach their own conclusion, even if it is 'I'm not sure.'

Farming did change a great deal while Victoria was Queen, but some things didn't change much at all – and farm workers were still relatively poorly paid in 1901. Britain depended much more on industry than farming by the time Victoria died.

HarperCollins*Publishers* 2019

Unit 6.3, Let's do it! question 1 asks pupils to use the evidence they have looked at in the unit to answer the question, *'Did the Victorians have fun in their spare time?'*.

This activity supports the skill of using evidence to reach a conclusion. To support pupils in answering this question, you could first discuss the steps below:

It almost doesn't matter which conclusion they come to with this question, it is how pupils **arrange** and **select the evidence** to support a conclusion that is important. The best answers might also suggest that many Victorians didn't have much spare time, or enough money to spend on fun.

Begin by showing the kinds of things Victorians did, many of which are included in this unit – sport, games, music, the fair, circuses and shows. Which ones would they choose to include in their answer? Which ones would they exclude? Which ones grew up specifically during Victorian times? Which were most important in Victorian times? Are there any that you could do without spending money, or were they all expensive?

Next, you might discuss whether any of these might be thought of as 'having fun,' both by us today and by the Victorians. How do we know that the Victorians thought them 'fun?' What evidence do we have to show this? The fact that they were very popular suggests that Victorians did, indeed, think of them as suitable activities for their enjoyment.

Ask them to use what they already know about Victorian times to think about different types of people – rich and poor, young and old, men and women, children, to see whether they all did the same kind of things to have fun. The Great Exhibition, for example, had cheaper admission prices on some days so ordinary people could attend. You could go to the fair and have fun even if you had very little or no money to spend.

Finally, they should reach a conclusion **based on the evidence they have used.** It is the way they have selected and used this evidence to support their conclusion that is important.

Unit 8.2, Let's do it!, question 2 asks *'How significant a person was Florence Nightingale?'*

To support pupils in answering this question, you could first discuss the steps below:

The first step in answering this question is to decide **how** to measure 'significance'. Pupils might find it easier if you use the term 'very special' or 'very useful'.

Ian Dawson, a well-known historian and history teacher, uses these criteria for deciding significance.

If it/a person:
- changed events at the time
- improved lots of people's lives – or made them worse
- changed people's ideas
- had a long-lasting impact on the country or the world
- had been a really good or a very bad example to other people of how to live or behave.

Are Ian Dawson's criteria helpful in this instance? Perhaps *'improved lots of people's lives'* might be a useful starting point. In what ways did Florence Nightingale improve life for the sick? Do any of the other criteria apply? You might broaden the discussion to include other ways Florence was important – perhaps as an inspiration to others?

The next step, once the criteria have been agreed, is to find out all the ways Florence Nightingale improved life for the sick. This includes making hospitals cleaner, improving training for nurses, writing books about how to be a nurse or how to run a hospital, bullying government ministers into making improvements, and so on.

After that, it is important to make a judgement as to how much all these actions improved things both at the time, and later.

Finally, pupils need to decide if all these things were directly a result of Florence Nightingale and her work, or were other people involved too. Only then can they decide whether they think she was a significant individual who had a huge impact on people in Victorian times.

Ancient Egypt

Topic introduction: Ancient Egypt

The history of people is also the history of good farmland – farmland to grow food, to produce surpluses, to use that wealth to make life better for everyone. Good farmland depends on water. Egypt's farmland is in a narrow belt either side of the River Nile, and throughout history the annual floods of the Nile have made Egypt's soil rich and fertile. Without the River Nile, there would have been no Ancient Egyptian civilisation.

The Nile was more than a supply of water – it was a highway linking Egypt to the outside world. Upstream lay Nubia and Central Africa, source of many of Egypt's raw materials. Beyond the Nile Delta lay the Mediterranean Sea and the rest of the known world. Utilising the Nile helped Egypt to grow and prosper over 3000 years until it was finally conquered by the Romans and became part of the Roman Empire.

Of course, it was the ordinary people who did all the work in the fields and building the pyramids and temples that Egypt is famous for. Life for many of them was hard. If the floods failed, droughts led to famine and many died. If the floods were good, huge crops were grown and the surplus could be both exported and stored for use in future years.

It was this surplus that allowed an elite to develop, and the pharaoh was the most important person of all. He – it was almost always a 'he' – decided policy, he planned wars of conquest, trading expeditions, temple and pyramid building. He could even, as in the case of Akhenaten, change the gods Egyptians believed in!

The Ancient Egyptians were very inventive, and their medicine was very advanced for the time. They rightly deserve their fame as one of the most powerful ancient civilisations. At one stage, Alexandria was the most important centre of learning in the whole world, and the pyramid at Giza was the biggest man-made structure in the world until Lincoln Cathedral was rebuilt around 1200 CE. Ancient Egypt deserves to be remembered for its great achievements.

Overview of Pupil Book contents

Unit	Content
1	Importance of the River Nile. Floods, drought and the delta. Where does the River Nile start? Is the Nile as important to Egypt today?
2	Ancient Egypt in time and place. The Old Kingdom, the Middle Kingdom and the New Kingdom. Decline of Egypt. What did pharaohs do all day?
3	Everyday life for rich and poor. What were Egyptian houses like? How was life different for rich and for poor? What crops did farmers grow? What other jobs did people do? How do we know?
4	What did Egyptian women do all day? What about the children? Did they go to school? What did they learn? How important was family to the Ancient Egyptians?
5	Life and death. Were all Egyptian tombs the same? Mummies and canopic jars. Were all Egyptians buried in pyramids? Why is the grave of Tutankhamun so important?
6	Trade and conquest. What different kind of boats did the Egyptians have? What did Egypt import and export? Which countries did they trade with? Did this trade make Egypt rich? How good was Egypt's army?
7	How inventive were the Egyptians? Famous Egyptian inventions. What happened when you became ill? How good were doctors in Ancient Egypt?
8	Why is the world so fascinated by Ancient Egypt? Should all the artefacts in museums around the world be returned to Egypt?
9	Looking at the wider picture: 1. History and Literacy – water 2. History and Science – mummification 3. Writing 4. Religion and beliefs

Knowledge organiser and skills grid

Knowledge organiser

Some key facts about Ancient Egypt:

- The River Nile was absolutely crucial to Egypt – without the river and its annual floods, there would have been no Ancient Egypt!
- Ancient Egypt was an important power for about 3000 years, until the Romans invaded and conquered Egypt around 30 BCE.
- The pharaoh was the most important person running the country – Egyptians thought of him as a god. A strong pharaoh made Egypt powerful; a weaker pharaoh often lost land and wealth to other countries.
- There were a few female pharaohs – Hatshepsut and Cleopatra are perhaps the most famous.
- Egypt's wealth came from its farmers. This allowed craftspeople and priests to spend time on other things.
- There were three seasons in each year – the Flood Season; the Growing Season and the Harvest Season. Most of the building work was done in the Flood Season.
- Egypt traded around the Mediterranean and the Persian Gulf, importing lots of luxuries for the rich and exporting food.
- Not all Egyptians were buried in pyramids.
- Egyptian doctors were in demand all over the ancient world.
- Egyptians had over 700 different pictures they used to represent words or sounds when writing.
- Egyptians had over 2000 different gods – they believed that you had to be very careful to keep on the good side of the gods and make offerings to the right god at the right time!
- Since the time of Napoleon, around 1800 CE, the rest of the world has been fascinated by life in Ancient Egypt.

Skills Grid

Unit	History skills targeted
Unit 1	Significance
Unit 2	Chronology and sense of period, utility of evidence
Unit 3	Using evidence to reach a conclusion
Unit 4	Interpretations, similarity and difference
Unit 5	Continuity and change
Unit 6	Comparing the army of Egypt with that of another history period
Unit 7	Making a convincing argument
Unit 8	Causation – why is the world so fascinated by Ancient Egypt?

Additional resources: Ancient Egypt

- Juliet Desailly, *Maat's Feather*, Book Guild Publishing
- Juliet Desailly, *Ammit's Revenge*, Book Guild Publishing
- Isobel and Imogen Grenberg, *Discover the Ancient Egyptians*, Frances Lincoln
- George Hart *Eyewitness: Ancient Egypt*, Dorling Kindersley
- Gill Harvey and Struan Reid *The Usborne Encyclopedia of Ancient Egypt*, Usborne.
- Fiona Macdonald, *Children in History – the Egyptians*, Franklin Watts
- Jacqueline Morley, *How would you survive as an Ancient Egyptian?*, Franklin Watts
- 'Teaching Ancient Egypt', *Primary History*, 67
- 'So Was Everyone an Ancient Egyptian?', *Primary History*, 73
- 'What made Cleopatra so special?', *Primary History*, 74
- Joan Fletcher, 'The Story of Egypt', (for teachers, based on the BBC TV Series of the same name)
- 10 Facts about Ancient Egypt, www.natgeokids.com and search 'Ancient Egypt'.
- A collection of materials and articles, www.historyonthenet.com and search 'Ancient Egyptians'
- 10 things you (probably) didn't know about Ancient Egypt, www.historyextra.com and search 'Ancient Egypt'.
- BBC Bitesize class clips, www.bbc.com and search 'Ancient Egypt KS2', then click 'Class clips'.
- Cat mummies discovered in tombs, news.sky.com/story/dozens-of-cat-mummies-discovered-in-ancient-egyptian-tombs-11551161
- www.ancient.eu/egypt/ (for teachers)
- Egyptian archaeology collection (replicas), www.tts-group.co.uk and search 'Egyptian Archaeo-Box'.
- Beliefs in Ancient Egypt Scheme of Work, www.history.org.uk and search 'Ancient Egypt scheme of work'.
- www.history.org.uk/primary/resource/8891/ancient-and-modern-making-sense-of-the-egyptians Ancient and Modern: Making sense of the Egyptians
- BBC Lost Lands – Ancient Egypt, www.bbc.co.uk and search title

Collins Big Cat books available at www.collins.co.uk:
- Collins Big Cat – *Discovering Tutankhamun's Tomb* (Emerald)
- Collins Big Cat – *Great Architects* (Copper)
- Collins Big Cat – *How to be an Ancient Egyptian* (Copper)

HarperCollins*Publishers* 2019

Getting better at history: Ancient Egypt

Making greater use of history's concepts and skills

History is not just about content, it is also a process of study and as pupils get better at history they ought to move away from an emphasis on content to an increasing emphasis on process – as, in the case below, why historians **differ** about the role of women in Ancient Egypt.

Unit 4.1 gives us two different views, or interpretations, about the role of women in Ancient Egypt:

> Although women in Ancient Egypt were not equal with men, they had many rights.

> 'Egyptian women had a free life, compared to her contemporaries in other lands. She wasn't a feminist, but she could have power and position if she was in the right class. She could hold down a job, or be a mother if she chose. She could live by herself or with her family. She could buy and sell to her heart's content. She could follow the latest fashions or learn to write if she had the chance… She helped her husband, she ran her household. She lived a similar life to that of her mother and grandmother… She was an ancient Egyptian woman with hopes and dreams of her own… not too much different from woman of today.'
>
> Caroline Seawright, *Egyptian Women: Life in Ancient Egypt*, © 2001,
> http://www.thekeep.org/~kunoichi/kunoichi/themestream/women_egypt.html

The key question here is not **how** they differ, but **why** they are different. The 'how' is easy to pick out.

Why do they differ? What evidence do the authors use to support their views? The first interpretation uses no evidence to support their assertion. Does that mean it is not true? What do we already know about the role of women that supports this statement? Are there things that we know that contradict this statement? Can we reach a meaningful conclusion about this interpretation from what we already know about the role of women in Egypt?

Caroline Seawright uses evidence to support her view – a woman could hold power, run the household, buy and sell, live on her own or with her family, much like women today. Do we know other evidence that **supports** this view? Or do we know evidence that **contradicts** this view? Do we agree with her interpretation?

Finally, which – if any – of these interpretations do we agree with, and why? We might prefer one or the other, or we might have a completely different view of our own. As long as we have evidence to support it then that is fine. It is perfectly possible for historians to have different views – it doesn't mean they are wrong!

Resource sheet: Unit 2.1 – Let's do it! question 1

Find out about Egyptian step pyramids, like the one built for King Djoser. How are they similar, and how are they different, to other pyramids found in Egypt?

	Similar to other pyramids	Different to other pyramids
When were they built?		
How big were they?		
What materials were used?		
What were they used for?		
Anything else …?		

Resource sheet: Unit 3.4 – Let's do it! question 2

As a class, make a list of questions you still have about everyday life in Ancient Egypt. Where might you find the answers to these questions?

Questions we still have about everyday life in Ancient Egypt	Where we might find the answer to this question?

Resource sheet: Unit 6.1 – Let's do it! question 1

Make a 'trade map' for Ancient Egypt, showing all the places mentioned in the text and that Egypt bought and sold goods with.

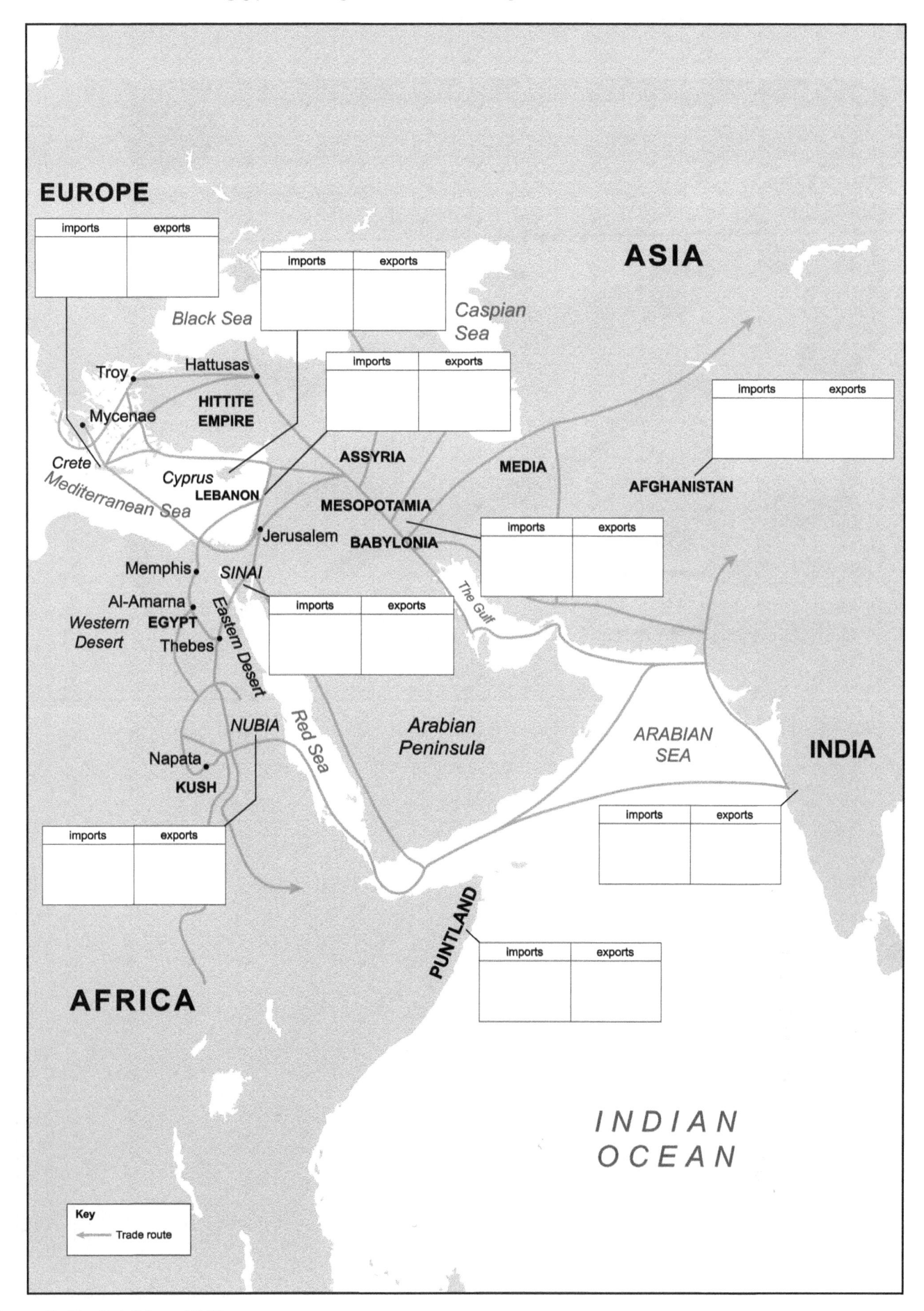

HarperCollins*Publishers* 2019

105

Resource sheet: Unit 7.2 – Let's do it! question 1

Look carefully at this collection of medical tools found in a tomb in Ancient Egypt. Are there any still in use today? Underneath the photograph draw the modern equivalent surgeons might use today.

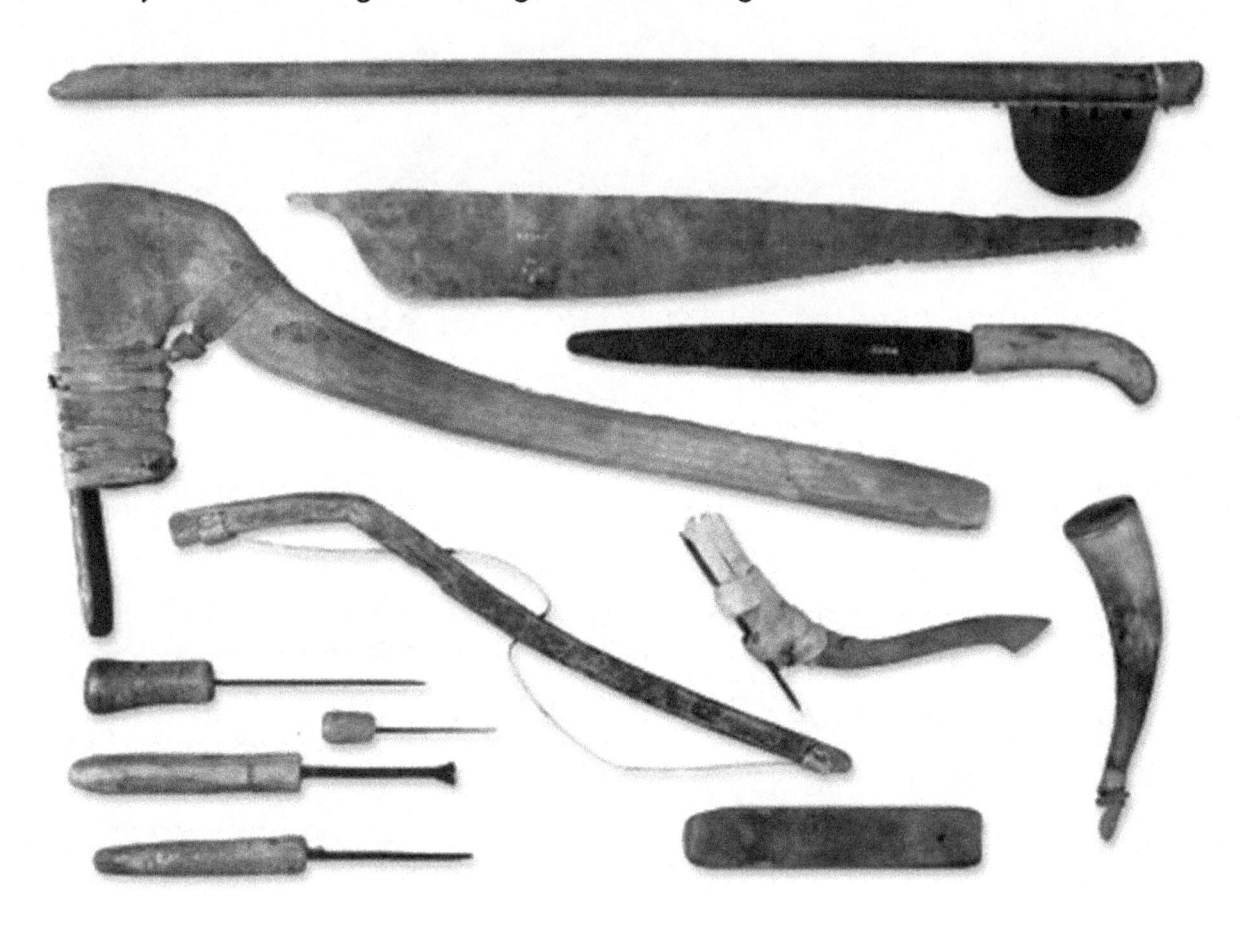

Pupil Book model answers

Unit 3.4, Think about it! question 3 asks *'How useful is this painting in telling us about rich people's houses?'*.

To support pupils in answering this question, you could first discuss the steps below:

When they have examined the evidence about the houses of rich people, and decided **which** evidence they trust, they are in a position to start to answer the question.

The painting might be very useful, quite useful, a little bit useful, or not at all useful, depending which evidence they believe to be accurate, and they will decide if it is accurate or not based on what they already know, or have found out, about Ancient Egypt, houses and homes, and life for the rich.

Key sentences might be something like, 'I think this picture is very useful in telling us about the houses of the rich because it shows exactly what the text tells us, (for example – high walls around the house; water to keep the place cool; flat roof for the house) and I found evidence from the time that agrees with this picture...'

Unit 6.2, Let's do it! question 4 asks *'How does the army of Ancient Egypt compare with other armies you have studied – for example, the Roman army?'*

This is an exercise in comparing different historical periods.

There are several different ways to answer this question. They might write a paragraph about the Egyptian army, then a paragraph about another army and finally making comparisons between the two.

Perhaps a more effective way is to write several paragraphs each on a different theme – weapons, uniforms, tactics, successful battles, for example – comparing each army in each paragraph. It is up to them. Pupils do need to know enough about **both** armies to make the comparison meaningful. A planning sheet like this might help.

	Egyptian army	another army
weapons	spear bow and arrow chariot	
tactics	siege chariot break through enemy lines lose as few men as possible	
successful battles	invasion of the Sea Peoples 1178 BCE	

Remember, weapons and tactics changed over time as the Egyptians adopted the chariot, and bronze then iron weapons. Ask: How are you going to include this in your answer?

Unit 8.3, Think about it! question 1 asks *'Do you think Egypt should be able to take back artefacts on display around the world?'*

This is an exercise in reaching a conclusion.

The best way to answer this question is with a balanced argument – yes and no – followed by a conclusion. Again, there is no one correct answer; it is how pupils marshal their argument and support that argument with evidence. The **way** the argument is structured will help you understand how much pupils have understood about the topic.

One way to answer this question might be like this:

Museums should be able to keep the artefacts that had been acquired legally, with the permission of the Egyptian authorities, because…

Some artefacts would have been lost forever if Britain and other countries had not rescued them…

People in other countries should be able to see what life was like in Ancient Egypt even if they can't afford to go there…

Museums should be made to return the artefacts because they belong to Egypt…

Many were stolen or taken illegally…

Now Egypt has the money and skills to preserve them properly…

People in Egypt should be able to see their own history…

In conclusion, *I* believe that… because…

Ancient Greece

Topic introduction: Ancient Greece

The history of Ancient Greece covers the period from the Trojan Wars around 1200 BCE until the Romans conquered Greece in 146 BCE. It is the story of city-states, such as Athens and Sparta, who were as often fighting each other as fighting invaders such as the Persians. They established colonies and traded all around, what was to them the known world – mostly around the Mediterranean and the Black Sea. These colonies made Greece very rich.

It is also the story of science and technology. Famous Greeks such as Pythagoras, Plato and Archimedes carefully observed the world around them and made discoveries in mathematics, science, philosophy and medicine. Some modern medical students still take the Hippocratic Oath ('to do no harm to patients') when they become doctors. Greek plays are still performed today in the theatre, and of course the Olympic Games originated in Ancient Greece.

Perhaps the greatest significance of the Ancient Greeks is the impact they have had on life today. In Athens around 500 BCE democracy began. The idea that everyone should have a say in government, (although in Athens this meant male citizens only) dates from that time. Trial by a jury of your peers, an essential part of the legal system in many countries today dates from Ancient Greek times. Greeks built the first lighthouse, in Alexandria; the first alarm clock; and the first water mill. People in the 18th and 19th centuries were fascinated by the Greeks and copied the 'Classical' style of their architecture. Buildings such as the British Museum were designed to look like Greek temples. Even the Romans copied Greek buildings and statues. No wonder people today still admire and study the Ancient Greeks.

Overview of Pupil Book contents

Unit	Content
1	Ancient Greece in time and place. Jason and the Argonauts. A Mediterranean climate. Chronology of Ancient Greece. Athens and city-states.
2	Everyday life – at home with a family. How much power did women have? Growing up in Ancient Greece. Sparta was different!
3	War on land and on sea. What was it like to be a Greek soldier? Fighting the Persians. War at sea. Athens v Sparta. How do we know? How important was war to the Ancient Greeks?
4	How did the Greeks explain the world they lived in? Why did they have so many gods? Visiting the Oracle at Delphi. Stories and myths.
5	Trade and empire. Where were the Greek colonies? How wealthy were they? The Pillars of Herakles and the edge of the Greek world. The importance of trade. Pytheas and his voyage of discovery.
6	Olympic Games – why was there so much emphasis on sport? Did the Olympic Games change over time? Sport for women – the Games of Heraea.
7	Culture – going to the theatre. Science and Medicine. Mathematics. Greek inventions. Who was the most significant Ancient Greek?
8	What did the Greeks do for us? How have the Ancient Greeks influenced the way we live today?
9	Looking at the wider picture: 1. Food 2. History and film 3. Alexander the Great 4. Clothes through the ages

Knowledge organiser and skills grid

Knowledge organiser

Some key facts about Ancient Greece:

- Ancient Greece was made up of lots of small city-states that spent a lot of time fighting each other as well as fighting other countries.
- Athens and Sparta were the two most powerful city-states.
- Ancient Greece was important for around 1000 years, from around 1200 BCE until it was conquered by Rome around 168 BCE.
- The Greeks had a powerful navy. They developed the trireme, a fast ship with three rows of oars, often having 180 rowers that could travel at 10 knots.
- The Greeks traded all around the Mediterranean Sea and into the Black Sea.
- The first Olympic Games were held in 776 BCE. At first there were only running races, but later more events were added. They were held every four years until they were banned by the Romans in 393 CE.
- Democracy began in Athens around about 500 BCE.
- Herodotus, the first historian, was born in Greece in 484 BCE.
- The Greeks loved stories and myths, and used them to explain the world they lived in. Some of these, such as Aesop's Fables, children still read today!
- Since the 18th century, many people have built houses and public buildings in the style of the Ancient Greeks – we call this the Neo-Classical style of building.
- Greeks loved going to the theatre. They built huge open-air theatres with thousands of seats. All the parts were played by men.

Skills grid

Unit	Skills
1	Chronology and sense of period
2	Similar and different, interpretations
3	Using evidence to reach your own conclusion
4	Presenting a researched piece of work
5	Causation, similar and different
6	Continuity and change
7	Significance
8	Reaching a reasoned judgement based on knowledge of Ancient Greece

Additional resources: Ancient Greece

- *Greek Myths*, retold by Heather Amery, Usborne
- Barry Cunliffe, *The extraordinary voyage of Pytheas the Greek*, (for teachers)
- Terry Deary and Martin Brown, *Horrible Histories: Groovy Greeks*, Scholastic Non Fiction
- Edith Hall, *Introducing the Ancient Greeks*, W.W. Norton (for teachers)
- Linda Honan, *Spend the Day in Ancient Greece*, Jossey-Bass
- Anne Pearson, *Eyewitness: Ancient Greece*, Dorling Kindersley
- Michael Wood, *In Search of the First Civilisations*, BBC Books (for teachers)
- 'Teaching the Ancient Greeks', *Primary History*, 71
- 'Wot, No Women? Did all Ancient Greek women stay at home and weave?', *Primary History*, 76
- Ashmolean Museum Oxford Greek gallery, www.ashmolean.org and search 'Greece'
- British Museum online guide to Ancient Greece, especially the section on the Olympic Games under 'Festivals and Games', www.ancientgreece.co.uk
- A history of the ancient Olympic games, including a list of the great athletes, is available at www.olympic.org. Select 'Ancient Games' from the bottom of the 'Olympic Games' tab.
- Scheme of Work: Ancient Greece, www.history.org.uk and search 'scheme of work Ancient Greece'.
- Lesson plans on Ancient Greek myths, www.history.org.uk and search 'Greek myths'
- What did the Ancient Greeks do for us? www.historyextra.com and search title.
- Trade in Ancient Greece (for teachers), www.ancient.eu/article/115/trade-in-ancient-greece/ and search title.
- www.timemaps.com/civilizations/ancient-greeks/ (for teachers)

Collins Big Cat books available at www.collins.co.uk:

- Collins Big Cat – *Ancient Greeks and Why They Matter to Us* (Sapphire)
- Collins Big Cat – *Great Greek Myths* (Sapphire)
- Collins Big Cat – *How to be an Ancient Greek* (Sapphire)

HarperCollins*Publishers* 2019

Getting better at history: Ancient Greece

Making greater use of history's concepts and skills

History is not just about content, it is also a process of study. As pupils get better at history they ought to move away from an emphasis on content to an increasing emphasis on process – **why** something happened rather than **what** happened, for example.

Unit 1.1: What can we learn about the Ancient Greeks from the story of Jason and the Golden Fleece?

Some children will take the story of Jason and the Argonauts at a simplistic level – it is made up so it doesn't tell us anything.

Better responses will seek parallels between the story and Greek life. For example, the Greeks were good sailors and often sailed to the end of the world. They loaded their ships with food and water and sailed away for several years at a time. Storms at sea were dangerous and ships were often lost or wrecked. On long voyages, sailors would tell tales to each other and these would sometimes become confused with what really happened. **Some** aspects of the story might be true, whereas **others** might not.

The best responses will go further, and draw links between the Greek wars and Jason's voyage, separating out what might be true from what is obviously made up. They will link Greek myths to the way the Greeks explained their world to themselves and agree that we can learn quite a lot about the Greek world from Jason's story. To do this, requires a very high level of historical skill.

Resource sheet: Unit 2.1 – Let's do it! question 1

Find out about the fruit and vegetables Greeks grew and ate. How similar, and how different, were they to what we grow and eat today? Fill in the table, then answer the questions below.

Eaten by the Ancient Greeks	Eaten by us today
bread	
cheese	

I think the foods eaten by the Ancient Greeks were:

☐ very similar

☐ quite similar

☐ a little different

☐ very different

to the foods we eat today. I think this because:

....

....

HarperCollins*Publishers* 2019

Resource sheet: Unit 6.2 – Let's do it! questions 1–2

Find out all the sports that were added to the Ancient Olympics over time. Fill in the table and then answer the questions below.

Original sports	Added by the Ancient Greeks	Part of the modern Olympics
Running	wrestling	
	javelin throwing	

How much continuity, and how much change, was there over the whole period of the Ancient Olympics?

....

....

How much continuity, and how much change, is there between the sports in the original Olympic Games and the modern games restarted in 1900?

....

....

What other changes have taken place?

....

....

Resource sheet: Unit 7.1–7.3 – Let's do it! question 1

Research each of the famous Ancient Greeks in this unit. Find out what each of them was famous for. Give each a score out of 10 in terms of significance.

Famous Greek	Why famous?	Score out of 10
Herodotus	wrote the first history book	7
Pytheas	explorer and geographer	8

I think the most significant Ancient Greek was ....

because ....

....

Resource sheet: Unit 8.3 – Let's do it! questions 1–2

What did the Greeks do for us?

Throughout this book, there have been lots of examples to show how the Ancient Greeks have had a big influence on modern-day life. Go back through the whole book and make a list of as many as you can. Sort your list into two – 'Big Impacts' and 'Smaller Impacts.' This should help you decide priorities. Finally sort each list into a rank order – put those with the biggest impact at the top of your list.

List of impacts	'Big impact'	'Smaller impact'

HarperCollins*Publishers* 2019

Pupil Book model answers

Unit 5.2, Think about it! question 2 asks *'In what ways is the Kyrenia similar to, and different from, a trireme?'*

This encourages pupils to consider similarity and difference.

There are details of a trireme in Unit 3.2 and the *Kyrenia* features in Unit 5.2.

It is relatively easy to pick out the **differences** between the two ships – size, shape (length and width), purpose, speed, cargoes, time away from home, size of the crew for example – are all clearly enumerated in the text.

The **similarities** are perhaps harder to list. Both ships used sails, were made of wood, had oars, (although the oars were for different purposes) and are typical of the Ancient Greek world.

The best answers will perhaps question how much we can tell from replicas – both the trireme and the *Kyrenia* are modern-day replicas, although they are based on wrecks found by archaeologists, so they should be similar. Archaeologists hope that by sailing the replica ships they can find out even more about them, how they were built and what they were used for.

In Unit 5.3, Let's do it! question 3, pupils are asked to write Pytheas' obituary.

To support pupils in writing the obituary, you could first discuss the steps below:

This is an exercise in research – in finding out information – and then presenting the results of that research in a disciplined structured way. You might begin by asking pupils to brainstorm what they think an obituary should contain. There is no correct answer to this question, although obviously the factual details ought to be accurate.

Obituaries usually include personal details, main achievements, why the person is famous, perhaps – but not very often – some criticism of the person who has died if they have done something unusual or wrong. But mostly an obituary speaks 'well of the dead'. A simple grid like this might help to research and structure an obituary:

Area of research	Findings
Personal life	• Born in Marseilles in 350 BCE
Main achievement	
Any controversies	
What people at the time said of him	
Anything else you think is important	

HarperCollins*Publishers* 2019

Unit 8.2, Let's do it! question 3 asks *'Do you think the Parthenon Marbles should be returned to Greece?'*

This is an exercise in reaching a conclusion. There is no one correct answer; it is how pupils marshal their argument and support that argument with evidence that matters. The **way** the argument is structured will help us understand how much pupils have understood about the topic. A similar question in the Egypt Teacher Notes explores a two-sided answer.

They could answer 'yes,' and structure an argument totally behind that idea, or 'no' in exactly the same way. You might hold a debate where pupils have to take sides and argue one side or the other.

Or, they might produce a 'yes', 'no', 'maybe' answer that looks at all sides of the question and finally comes to a conclusion.

One way to answer this question might be like this:

> **Lord Elgin** brought the marbles back to England around 1801–1812. He said he had permission from the Ottoman Government (who ruled Greece at the time) to remove the marbles. Marble sculptures that fell off the Parthenon at the time were being used by local people to make lime. The Parthenon was a very famous monument in Athens. Lord Elgin thought the sculptures would be destroyed if he left them in Athens. In 1815, Lord Elgin sold the marbles to the British Government who then gave them to the British Museum, where they now attract many tourists every year.
>
> It is also argued that **if** the marbles were returned to Athens they would be ruined by air pollution and acid rain. The argument says they would be safer for posterity if they stay in the special gallery built for them in the British Museum in the 1930s.
>
> If the British Museum gave back the Elgin Marbles, that might lead to every piece of Ancient Greek remains being returned to Greece even if, as Lord Elgin argued, it had been legally moved. Where do you stop?
>
> I think the Elgin Marbles should stay in the British Museum where they belong, are safe, and can be viewed by millions of visitors every year.

The Maya

Topic introduction: The Maya

The Maya were a Stone Age society from Meso (Central) America. They first appeared around 2000 BCE but gradually spread across Central America. They adapted well to the rainforest environment and became rich and powerful. They were in some ways like the Ancient Greeks – lots of separate city-states, often fighting each other. Strong leaders expanded the area they controlled, and weak rulers lost land. Some Maya cities were big, with populations of 50,000 or more. They were totally dependent on farming for their wealth, growing a variety of crops and sending them to market in the cities.

Some goods, such as salt and obsidian, were traded over long distances. Despite being a Stone Age society (with no access to metals), they were very inventive. They could predict eclipses, built their pyramids and temples aligned with equinoxes, had a written language (some of which we still cannot translate) and an advanced numerical system. But around 900 CE something strange happened. Up to 95 per cent of the Maya population 'disappeared' from their cities.

Historians disagree about why this happened. Many people think the Maya were the most advanced society in America. Perhaps they were too successful? Drought and/or deforestation probably played a big part in what is a big history mystery. Archaeologists now think that many of the Maya moved into Yucatan in Northern Mexico where water supplies were more secure, but no one is really certain.

The Maya make a perfect contrast with Stone Age Britain (lots of similarities, but also many differences) and also Egypt (pyramids and hieroglyphs) or Shang China (jade and obsidian). They are also frequently in the news as more and more ruins are discovered in the rainforest and jungle. There are also around 7 million Maya living in the area today – some still in the traditional way – and these give us a special insight into the lives of the Maya so long ago.

Overview of Pupil Book contents

Unit	Content
1	Lost in the jungle! How explorers discovered the remains of Maya cities. Where – and when – did the Maya live, and what else was happening in the world at the same time?
2	What can we tell about the Maya from the 7 million Maya who live in the area today? Learning from the lives of the Maya who still live in a traditional way. The impact of tourism on the Maya.
3	What is it like living in the rainforest? Why is water a problem? How was chocolate grown, and what did the Maya do with it? Why was the rainforest so important to the Maya?
4	Maya cities – were they all the same? What was it like living in a Maya city of 50,000 people? Which were the most important buildings and people? Why did the Maya spend so much time fighting each other? Was the Maya 'ball game' the same as football?
5	Travel and trade – the interdependence of city and countryside. How did the Maya move goods around their lands? What was it like living in the country, and how do we know? Were the Maya an urban society, or a rural one?
6	How inventive were the Maya? What can we discover about them from their calendars, maths, science, writing, religion, and beliefs? Why did the Spanish try to remove all traces of the Maya?
7	What happened to the Maya around 900 CE? Did they 'disappear' or 'descend' to the Lowlands? Why are we not sure exactly what happened? Is there a lesson for us today in what happened to the Maya?
8	Bringing the story up to date – what were the consequences of the Spanish invasion in the 16th century? The story of Gonzalo Guerrero – the Spanish sailor who fought for the Maya. Why should we remember the Maya?
9	Looking at the wider picture: 1. History and Geography – how does the geography of the area help us to understand the lives of the Maya? 2. Pyramids across the globe – are they all the same? 3. Comparing Stone Age societies around the world.

Knowledge organiser and skills grid

Knowledge organiser

Some key facts about the Maya:

- 200 years ago, hardly anyone knew anything about the history of the Maya – their cities were ruins hidden in the jungles of Central America.
- Like the Greeks, the Maya lived in lots of separate city-states, often fighting each other. A strong leader made a city richer and more powerful – a weak leader lost wealth and land.
- Many of the Maya lived in tropical rainforest.
- Cocoa and lots of other foods we now eat came from the region.
- The Maya built pyramids too – many were over 20 metres tall.
- The Maya played a kind of football, except you could not use your hands or your feet – although historians disagree about many of the rules of the game.
- Although they had no wheeled transport or animals to pull them, the Maya built roads of crushed stone (called sacbe) linking the Maya world together.
- Some Maya cities had 50,000 people living in them – they relied on neighbouring farmers to bring food into the city markets every day.
- The Maya had over 160 different gods.
- The Maya had over 800 different hieroglyphs representing words or sounds. Historians still cannot read some of their writing!
- Around 900 CE many of the Maya cities were deserted. No one is really certain what happened to all those people. There are lots of different ideas put forward by historians.
- In 1517, the Spanish began to conquer the Maya. Many died from European diseases such as measles and smallpox. Maya cities were destroyed, and many buildings pulled down. The Spanish used the stones to build their own buildings.
- The Maya were a really successful Stone Age society.
- There are still around 8 million people of Maya descent living in Meso-America today – some still living in a traditional way.

Skills grid

Unit	History skills targeted
1	Chronology, sense of period
2	Continuity and change
3	Significance
4	Use of evidence, interpretations
5	Similarity and difference, reaching a conclusion
6	Writing a focused account, presenting conclusion
7	Cause and consequence, interpretations
8	Using historical knowledge to reach a conclusion

HarperCollins*Publishers* 2019

Additional resources: The Maya

- Ben Ballin and Alf Wilkinson, *B2F The Maya*, Wildgoose Publications
- Sheri Bell-Rehwoldt, *Amazing Maya Inventions you can build yourself*, Nomad Press
- 'The Maya: A 4,000 year old civilisation in the Americas', *Primary History*, 68
- Linda Lowery and Richard Keep, *The Chocolate Tree – A Mayan Folktale*, Lerner Books.
- BBC Lost Lands – The Maya. Available at www.bbc.co.uk
- The Maya today, nationalgeographic.org/media/modern-day-maya/
- Were the Mayas the ultimate ancient civilisation? www.telegraph.co.uk and search 'Maya ancient civilisation'.
- The website of Dr Diane Davies, mayaarchaeologist.co.uk/
- Maya codices, www.maya-3d.com and click 'Reconstructions'
- Website devoted to the Maya ball game, www.mesoballgame.org
- Tours of Maya cities, photographs and descriptions, www.mesoweb.com
- Maya creation myth, www.youtube.com/watch?v=Jb5GKmEcJcw
- The Maya Mathematical System, www.mayacalendar.com
- Mexicolore website, www.mexicolore.co.uk/
- The BBC History website has a good section on the Maya, www.bbc.co.uk/history

Collins Big Cat books available at www.collins.co.uk:
- Collins Big Cat – *Chocolate: from Bean to Bar* (Copper)
- Collins Big Cat – *The Maya* (Pearl)

Getting better at history: The Maya

Developing a wider, more detailed and chronologically secure knowledge of the Maya

A wider, more detailed knowledge of the Maya

At the end of Unit 1 in this book we ask the pupils to brainstorm what they already know about the Maya, after studying the first unit. We also ask them to produce a list of questions they would like answered about the Maya. Return to these lists at the end of Unit 8 and ask the pupils to look again at their initial list of knowledge, and ask whether they still think it is accurate. It might be the case that some of the things they thought they knew they might now think inaccurate. In any case, they should be able to add much more detail to their understanding of the Maya and the way they lived. The extent of the added knowledge will give you a good indication as to how much wider and secure their knowledge of the Maya is.

A better chronological understanding of the Maya

You can undertake a similar task to see how their understanding of the chronology of the Maya has developed. Unit 1.3 asks pupils to draw a timeline from 4000 BCE to 2000 CE, marking on it all the dates relating to the Maya. You could ask pupils to return to this timeline, and ask them what is missing. After studying the Maya throughout this book, they should be able to add lots more examples. The number and sophistication of the examples they add to their own timeline will give you a clear indication of the extent to which their understanding of the Maya has developed throughout their studies.

Resource sheet: Unit 1.3 – Let's do it! questions 1–2

Carefully add all the dates you already know that relate to the Maya to the timeline. In another colour, add all the non-Maya dates from Unit 1. Next, add any other dates you know from your history lessons.

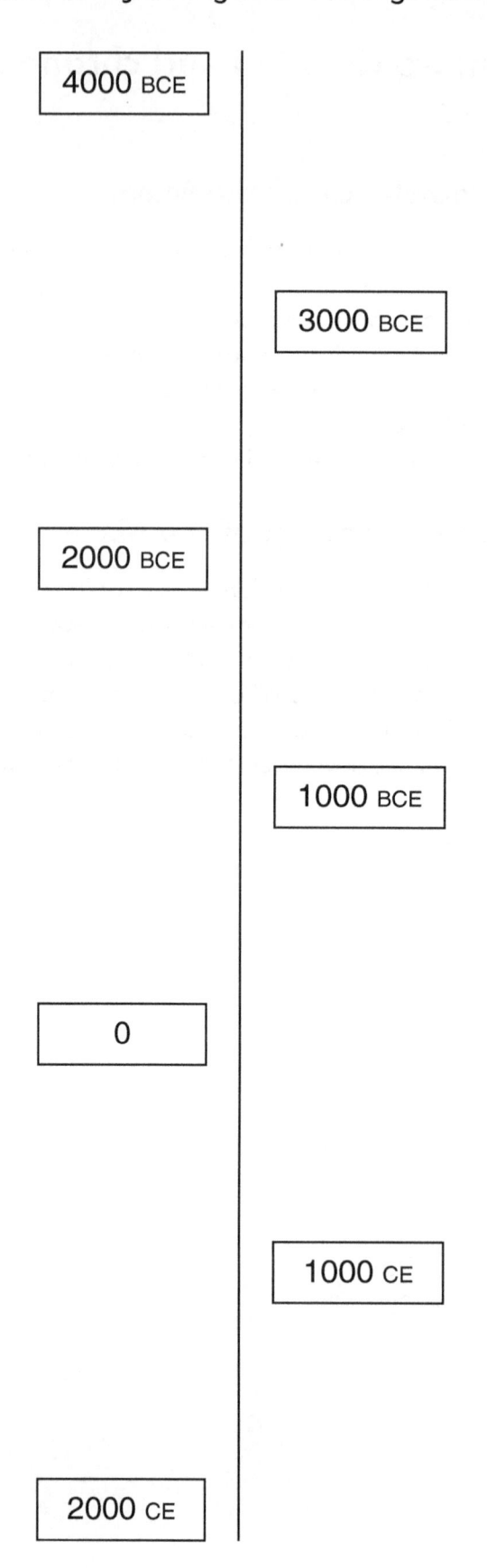

- 4000 BCE
- 3000 BCE
- 2000 BCE
- 1000 BCE
- 0
- 1000 CE
- 2000 CE

Resource sheet: Unit 2.3 – Think about it! question 2

Unit 2 has looked at how some of the Maya live today, often in a way that is quite traditional. Look back over Units 2.1 and 2.2. Fill in the table with all the aspects of Maya life you have discovered.

Traditional way of life	Modern way of life

Resource sheet: Unit 3.1 – Let's do it! question 1

Use the information you have discovered in Units 2 and 3 to complete the Maya family calendar. For each month, decide what a Maya family might be doing.

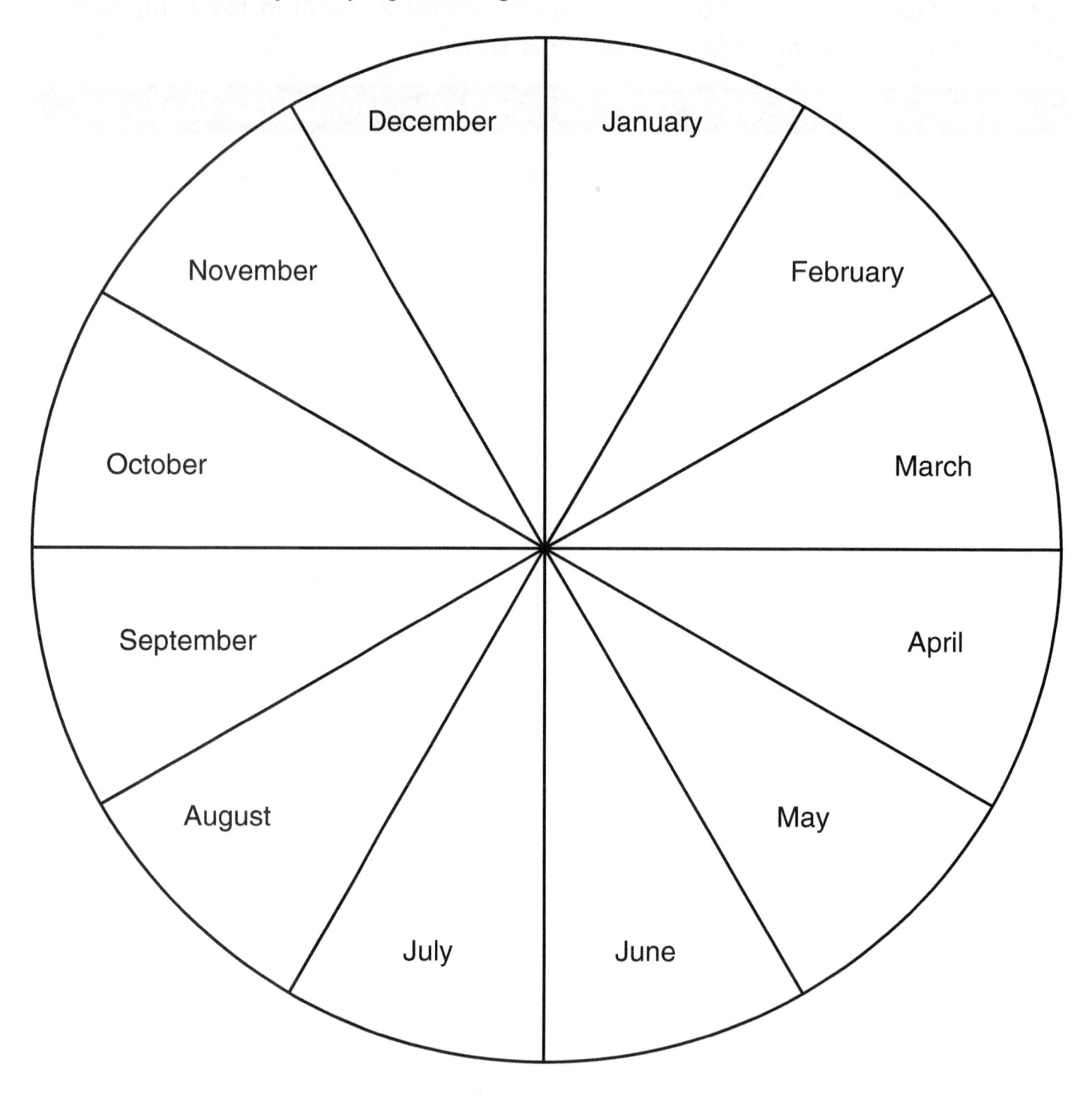

HarperCollins*Publishers* 2019

Resource sheet: Unit 5.3 – Let's do it! question 1

In each circle, list all the reasons you have discovered so far that explain whether the Maya were an 'urban' or 'rural' society. If a reason might fit in both circles, write it in the area where the circles overlap. If a reason does not fit into these categories, write it outside the circles.

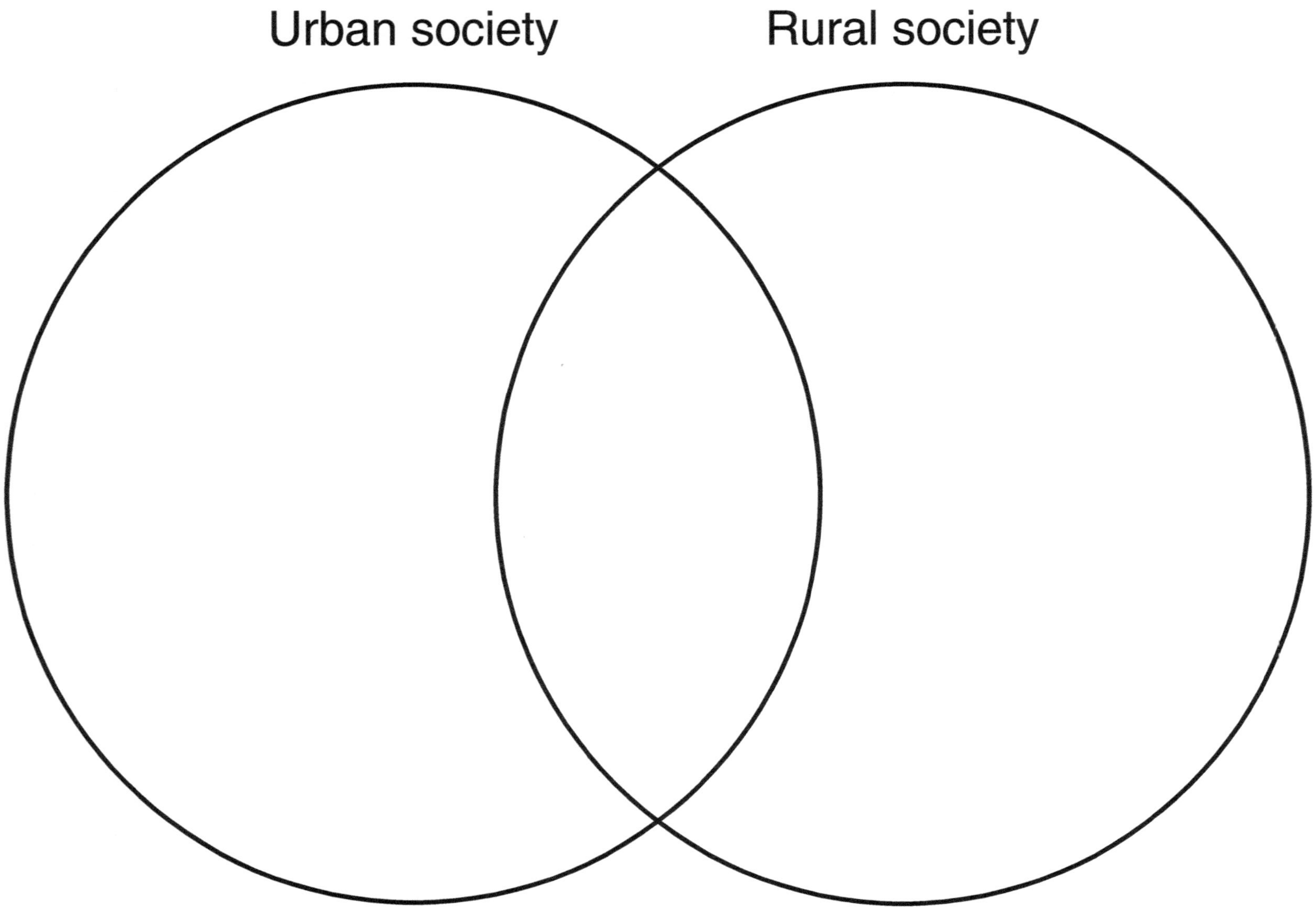

Rural society

Urban society

HarperCollins*Publishers* 2019

131

Resource sheet: Unit 6.3 – Let's do it! question 3

Do you think the Maya were inventive? Answer the questions below.

The Maya were inventive because:
Also they could:
However, very few Maya could read and write
And they didn't know how to use metal
So I think: Because:

Resource sheet: Unit 7.2 – Let's do it! question 1

Look carefully again at historians' suggestions as to what happened to the Maya (Unit 7.1 and your own research). Sort the information you have into the table below.

Cause	Consequence

Resource sheet: Unit 8 – Let's do it! question 2

Look carefully at these two images. Both images are of fighting men. Which is the Spanish conquistador, and which is the Maya warrior? How can you tell?

Use the two images to complete the table. An example has been added to help you:

Similarities	Differences
They both have weapons	

Which one would you expect to win in a fight? Why?

....

....

....

....

Pupil Book model answers

Unit 3.3, Let's do it! questions 2 and 3 ask pupils to hold a class discussion about the significance of the rainforest to the Maya.

To support pupils in creating their presentation, you could first discuss the steps below:

The first step in answering this question is to decide **how** to measure 'significance'. Pupils might find it easier if you use the term 'very special' or 'very useful'.

Ian Dawson, a well-known historian and history teacher, uses these criteria for deciding significance.

> If it/a person:
> - changed events at the time
> - improved lots of people's lives – or made them worse
> - changed people's ideas
> - had a long-lasting impact on the country or the world
> - had been a really good or a very bad example to other people of how to live or behave.

Are Ian Dawson's criteria helpful in this instance? Perhaps *'improved lots of people's lives'* might be a useful starting point. In what ways did the rainforest improve life for the Maya? Do any of the other criteria apply?

You might broaden the discussion to include other ways that the rainforest was important – perhaps as a source of food, or building materials, or chocolate?

The next step, once the criteria have been agreed, is to find out all the ways the Maya made use of the rainforest. Timber for building is very important – especially the sapodilla tree. Fruits and other foods were harvested from the forest. Clearing the rainforest revealed fertile soils and of course the cacao tree grew in the forest under the canopy. Also hunting in the forest provided most of the meat in the Maya diet.

Next, you might consider the negative aspects of the rainforest as a place to live. It is very wet for much of the year, and difficult to travel through. The soil, while fertile to begin with, loses its fertility after a few years so people have to move to new fields and clear more forest. Are there others you or the class can think of? The hilly terrain, for example?

Finally, pupils need to reach their own conclusion. Was the rainforest significant? Could the Maya have lived as well in the area if it was, say, desert or grasslands? What was specific about the rainforest that made it so important to the Maya – and to us today?

Of course, there is no one definite answer to this question – it all depends where pupils place the emphasis in their discussion, but their conclusion does need to be supported by the evidence they use.

Unit 4.3, Let's do it! question 1 asks *'Do you agree with Alex Woolf that all Maya cities were built in the same way?'*

To support pupils in answering this question, you could first go through the steps below.

A typical Maya city. Get pupils to describe or draw a typical Maya city. Pyramids, temples and a big square were in the centre. The square would double as a market place as well as a place of celebration. Remember the temples and pyramids would be covered in white plaster and probably red paintings. If, like Tikal, 60,000 people lived there, the place would be teeming with people going about their daily business.

Cities over time. Some Maya cities like El Mirador were important around the year 0, Tikal grew around 600 CE; and Chichen Itza and Mayapan were at their peak later. Even though they were built at different times, they were quite similar in design.

HarperCollins*Publishers* 2019

The case of Tulum. Tulum was built next to the sea, as a port, and is one of the smallest Maya cities, with a population of around 1500. It was surrounded by a wall which was 7 metres thick, 5–7 metres high, and nearly 800 metres long, with only five narrow gateways allowing entry. It was also one of the last to be built, and was most important around 1200–1300 CE.

Conclusion: Does the example of Tulum prove or disprove Alex Woolf's statement? Tulum is small, it is on the coast, it is surrounded by a wall that limits entry and exit – how typical is that? Or do we just not know enough about all Maya cities to be sure? Again, there is no definite answer to this question – although you could argue that **most** Maya cities were designed and built to a similar pattern.

Unit 7.2, Let's do it! question 1 challenges pupils to decide what they think happened to the Maya around 900 CE.

This exercise supports pupils to study and assess interpretations. To support pupils in answering this question, you could first go through the steps below:

First, how do we know what happened in the past? What evidence is there, and where does it come from? How reliable is it? Our picture of the Maya depends on all this evidence and our assessment of how useful it is. Get pupils to compile all the evidence they can about events around 900 CE and then decide which evidence they think is most useful for answering this question.

Next, look at the six interpretations that historians have come up with in the text book (page 41). Which do pupils think is most likely? What evidence is there to support that view? Which do they think is least likely? What evidence is there to support that view? There is no definitive answer!

Next, is it likely that only one of these causes on its own would cause such a catastrophe for 7 million people? Might there be more than one cause? Do they believe the 'Great Collapse' theory, that 95 per cent of the population disappeared; or the 'Great Descent' theory that most moved to rural areas and new cities in Yucatan? Can they find evidence to support either or both of these theories?

Finally, encourage pupils to come up with their own interpretation about what happened to the Maya around 900 CE, and ask them to provide the evidence to support their idea.

Some interpretations are more likely than others. For instance archaeologists and scientists are now convinced that there was a long drought at the time, which would have had serious effects on the Maya and their ability to grow enough food to feed everyone. Perhaps, after all, the Maya became just too successful?

Unit 8.1, Think about it! question 1 asks 'Imagine you are one of those Maya in the canoe in 1502, and you meet Columbus and his ship. What would you think? How would you feel? What would you say? What would you tell your friends when you got home?'

This encourages the development of a sense of period.

One of the hardest things for children to acquire in history is a sense of period – what was it really like to live at the time. This question will help you see whether or not your pupils have developed this.

In the Maya canoe. What were the Maya doing in the canoe? Where were they going? How was it moved through the sea? How big was the canoe? How many crew were there?

Meeting the Spanish ship. How big was the Spanish ship compared to the canoe? How was it similar to the canoe, and how was it different? Looking carefully at both images will help answer many of these questions.

Contact with the Spanish. Would you be afraid of the strangers, or welcoming? How would you communicate with them? What would you say? What would you have to offer the Spanish, and what might they have that you might want? Would you want to fight the strangers, or move away quickly because you were scared? If you had never met people like this before, how would you react?

Remember the way the Maya lived – the tools they had, the weapons they used, where they were going and why? All this would dictate how the Maya would respond. Again, there is no definite answer – we have no written accounts of how the Maya reacted on contact with the Spanish, but we need to make sure that there are no anachronisms – that actions and responses from the Maya are typical of the way the Maya lived at the time, not the way we live today.